The Book of Sports Lists 2

Also by David Brown (with Craig Brown)
The Book of Sports Lists

David Brown

THE BOOK OF SPORTS LISTS 2

WEIDENFELD AND NICOLSON · LONDON

To Mark McGreevy and Andrew Ramsey

Published in Great Britain by
George Weidenfeld & Nicolson Limited
91 Clapham High Street
London SW4 7TA

British Library Cataloguing in Publication Data is available.

ISBN 0 297 81136 3

Typeset by Deltatype Limited, Ellesmere Port
Printed in Great Britain by
The Guernsey Press Co. Ltd, Guernsey, C.I.

Contents

A
10 Sporting *Accolades*
Ages of 7 Great Cricketers when they Retired
15 *Ages* They'll Be in the Year 2000
7 Extraordinary Facts about *Edwin Boaler Alletson*'s Only Hundred
10 Milestones in *Athletics* History

B
3 Displays of *Bad Sportsmanship*
3 Stars who have Experienced *Bad Times*
10 Early Golfing Stages of *Severiano Ballesteros*
The last 7 *Balls* of the Most Exciting Test Match ever Played
4 Excuses for Anti-Social *Behaviour*
An Impossible Number of People to Count who like a *Bet*
5 Facts *Ian Botham* would rather Forget
5 *Brave* Sportsmen
8 Sports Stars who are not Desperately *Bright*
David Brown's List of Top Ten Sports Broadcasters

C
4 Sporting *Cheats*
3 Sporting *Coincidences*
The Radio Three Test Match Special *Commentary Team*
9 The Counties who Contested the First Cricket *County Championship* in 1873
10 Amusing *Cricketing Anecdotes*

D
10 Pieces of Information to help you to become a *Darts Bore*
5 Little known Eastern Bloc *Defectors*
5 Unusual *Diets*
15 Stars who Liked a *Drink*
3 Stars who Admitted to Taking *Drugs*
8 Current Professional Cricketers who went to *Durham University*

E

7 Sporting *Eccentrics*
11 Sportsmen who have met Unfortunate *Ends*
7 Sportsmen who have *Enjoyed Themselves*
7 Bizarre Pre-Match Soccer *Entertainments* Witnessed by Michael Coffey (Roving Football Fan)
3 Important *Events* in the Cricket World in 1864

F

4 Notorious Incidents which have called into Question the Ethic of *Fair Play*
12 *Fanatical* Sports Fans
10 of the Best Named Football *Fanzines*
8 Sportsmen's *Fathers' Occupations*
9 Unlikely Cricketing *Feats*
14 Sporting *Films*
3 Notable *Firsts*
Football League Division One 1965–6 – The Final Placings
Football League Division Four 1965–6 – The Final Placings
8 Sets of Personalities who are 'Not the Best of *Friends*'

G

6 Interesting Facts about *W. G. Grace*
9 *Gifts* Given by Sportsmen

H

5 *Headlines* concerning Tony Knowles, Snooker Player
3 *Hefty* goalkeepers
6 Sportsmen who Acted *Honourably*
10 Interesting *Horse Racing* Facts
6 Mixed *Humorous* Sporting Anecdotes

I

4 Sporting *Insults*

K

9 Cricketers who were *Killed* during the Great War

L

6 *Left-Wingers* who Played Football for London Clubs and have played Test Match Cricket
8 Cases of Extreme Bad *Luck*

M

5 Unusual Facts about Boxer *Terry Marsh*
5 Places that have witnessed Embarrassing *Mistakes*
4 Sportsmen who are Careful with their *Money*

N

5 of the *Nastiest* NFL Players
17 of the Better *Nicknames*
12 Unkind *Nicknames*
5 Stars who have Said *No*

O

7 Good Reasons for not Going to *Oklahoma University* to play Football
The 10 *Oldest* Cricketers to have Captained their Country for the first time in an Ashes Encounter
4 *Origins* of Indoor Games

P

14 *Personalities* who got it Wrong
9 Facts about the Great *Phar Lap*
3 Sportsmen who are *Pleased with Themselves*
5 American Footballing US *Presidents*
The Crimes for which 8 Stars were sent to *Prison*
4 Successful *Punts* by Professional Gambler Alex Bird
7 Famous Missed *Putts*

Q

16 Memorable Sporting *Quotations*

R

7 Events *Racing* would rather Forget
10 Cricketing *Ranks* in the Second World War
7 Stages in the *Relationship* between Hana Mandlikova and Jan Sedlak

6 Sportsmen with *Religious Leanings*
10 of the *Richest Prizes* in Sport
10 Stages in the *Romance* of Mike Tyson and Robin Givens
10 Examples of Early *Royal Involvement* with Horse Racing
The last 10 *Rugby League* Championship Winners
11 Important Dates in the History of *Rugby League*

S

6 Prolific *Sexual Athletes*
7 Sports People who think Sport is taken too *Seriously*
8 Instances of Taking the whole thing Much too *Seriously*
Gary Sobers' 6 *Sixes*
10 of the most Popular *Soccer Songs*
9 Sports Starts on their *Sport*
The 5 *Stages* in the Mary Decker/Zola Budd Incident – 3,000 Metres Final, Los Angeles Olympics, 1984
4 Stars who have *Suffered* in Car Crashes or from Disabilities
6 Sportsmen who found *Success* Early
7 Cricketing *Suicides*

T

The 4 Olympic Medallists to have played *Tarzan* in the Movies
6 Incidents that were not to Everybody's *Taste*
4 Historic Sporting *Telegrams*
3 Reasons why Sportsmen have lost their *Temper*
12 Sportsmen Discuss *Themselves*
6 Test Bowlers who have been No-Balled for *Throwing*
Alex Bird's 10 *Tips* to the Betting Man
11 English Cricketing *Tourists* of the United States and Canada in 1859
2 Dreadful Football British *Tragedies* in the 1980s
4 Quotes of *Lee Trevino*

U

8 *Unfortunate* Stories that hit the Football Pages in 1971–2
7 *Unlikely* Dismissals
6 *Unusual* Sporting Events
The 8 Items Dickie Bird Keeps in his *Umpire's Coat* and their Uses
11 Pieces of Completely *Useless Information*

W
The *Wilson* Family Tree

Y
10 *Yorkshire-Born Cricketers* who have played for another County

Z
And 1 *Zany* Story to end with

Acknowledgements

For their help and encouragement I would like to thank Mike Coffey, John Dowling, my brother Jamie and my former editor Martin Corteel, and all the regulars at the The Lobster Pot, West Malling.

10 Sporting Accolades

1 **'He was like a Ferrari and made us look like Chevrolets.'**

US golfer Tom Kite's description of Seve Ballesteros after the 1980 US Masters.

2 **'If I ever had an eight-foot putt and everything I owned depended upon it, I'd want Arnold Palmer to take it.'**

Bobby Jones, US golfer.

3 **'After horses he had ridden appear to have had hard races, they come back to me as if they had never had a race at all.'**

Peter Walwyn, racehorse trainer, on Irish jockey Pat Eddery.

4 **'Lestor Piggott is the best jockey in the world, the best judge of the form book and the greatest judge of his own races.'**

Alex Bird, professional punter.

5 **'He had the opposition so frightened they'd have a man marking him when they were warming up before the kick-off.'**

The great Bill Shankly once said this of the Preston and England winger, Tom Finney.

6 **'Benaud is just about the nearest thing there has been to a perfect captain.'**

Dickie Bird on Australian cricket captain, Richie Benaud.

7 **'I know we can beat England, but we just can't cope with Botham. He's a one man army.'**

Australian cricket captain, Kim Hughes, 1981.

8 'The little Argentinian is out on his own as the number-one player in the world.'

Footballer Ian Rush on Diego Maradona, 1987.

9 'Ben Crenshaw has the best grip, the best stance and the best swing I've ever seen. Besides that he's nice.'

Lee Trevino, US golfer, 1979.

10 'Ray Illingworth was the most honest and uninhibited of any captain with whom I have toured.'

Brian Johnston, cricket broadcaster.

Ages of 7 Great Cricketers when they Retired

1	Dr W. G. Grace	58
2	Willy Quaife	56
3	Wilfred Rhodes	52
4	Frank Woolley	51
5	Sir Jack Hobbs	51
6	Patsy Hendren	49
7	Percy Holmes	46

15 Ages They'll Be in the Year 2000

1	Severiano Ballesteros (golfer)	43
2	Eric Bristow (darts player)	43
3	Robin Cousins (ice skater)	43
4	Steve Davis (snooker player)	43

5	Jayne Torvill (ice skater)	43
6	Martina Navratilova (tennis player)	44
7	Björn Borg (tennis player)	44
8	Sebastian Coe (athlete)	44
9	Pele (footballer)	50
10	Alex Higgins (snooker player)	51
11	Tom Watson (golfer)	51
12	Muhammad Ali (boxer)	58
13	Bobby Charlton (footballer)	63
14	Lestor Piggott (jockey)	65
15	Henry Cooper	66

7 Extraordinary Facts about Edwin Boaler Alletson's Only Hundred

1 Alletson was scarcely more than a Nottinghamshire squad player.

2 In his nine years at Trent Bridge he only averaged 18.

3 On 20 May 1911, Alletson batting in a match against Sussex had scored 47 not out in fifty minutes.

4 His last-wicket partnership with Riley added 142 runs in forty minutes (Riley made ten).

5 Alletson went from 47 to 100 in about sixteen minutes.

6 He went from 100 to 189 in about twenty-four minutes.

7 One of his sixes had to be prized out of the woodwork of the new stand.

10 Milestones in Athletics History

1 3800 BC
Earliest evidence of organized running at Memphis in Egypt. Races were held between two pillars about 800 metres apart and were normally of four lengths.

2 490 BC
The famous run to Athens by Pheidippides and the subsequent Battle of Marathon.

3 1530
The first international athletics match between England and Scotland.

4 1866
The first English national championship organized by the Amateur Athletics Club at Beaufort House, Wellington Green, London.

5 1896
The birth of the modern Olympics, held in Athens. Appropriately, a Greek, Spiridon Louis, wins the marathon.

6 1914
This year sees the first technical rules for international competitions and the first list for world records, which were presented at the third International Amateur Athletic Federation Congress (IAAF formed in July 1912).

7 1936
The Berlin Olympics introduces the first official Olympic film, and the torch was seen by 150,000 viewers in twenty-eight halls in and around Berlin.

8 1960
Electronic boards are used for field events for the first time at the Rome Olympics.

9 1972
This year saw the fateful Munich Olympics. The games were severely scarred, if not to say ruined by terrorism. Dope testing was used for the first time. There was a record number of competitors: 1,599 from 122 nations.

10 1975

The IAAF introduced automatic suspensions for athletes found to have used anabolic steroids.

3 Displays of Bad Sportsmanship

1 **'Not many batsmen put themselves in that position'**
During the second test match at Christchurch, New Zealand in 1978, New Zealand fast bowler Ewan Chatfield ran up to bowl to Geoff Boycott. Without warning he whipped off the bails as Derek Randall started backing up and startled umpire Fred Goodall was obliged to give him out.

It was an unforgivable act of bad sportsmanship and New Zealand captain, Mark Burgess, hardly improved the atmosphere with the unnecessary remark that 'not many batsmen put themselves in that position'. The appropriate course of action would have been to stop in the delivery stride and hold the ball over the bails as a warning not to leave the crease prematurely again.

2 **Slow play**
In August 1967, Warwickshire needed 142 runs in 102 minutes to beat Yorkshire in a County Championship cricket match.

Unfortunately, Yorkshire used every trick in the book to waste time. They bowled only two overs in the last eleven minutes.

There was a hearing and the Yorkshire captain, Brian Close, refused to apologise. In fact, he made no secret that he would do the same again in similar conditions.

Close was at this time a very successful England captain. A week later he was not selected as captain of the MCC party to tour the West Indies that winter.

3 **Swift kick**
When the Pakistanis toured Australia in 1982, Australian fast bowler, Dennis Lillee, was fined $200 and suspended for two matches for kicking Javed Miandad after the equally controversial Pakistani batsman had knocked Lillee off balance when completing a single.

3 Stars who have Experienced Bad Times

1 **Kirk Stevens**
In early 1985 the long-haired, smiling, fit-looking Canadian, Kirk Stevens, was ranked fourth in the snooker world. He then fell on bad times, became a drug addict and lost all his money. In 1989 he was ranked seventy-eighth in the world. In November of that year he said: 'I've been in debt for five years and the tax man is being as patient as he can be. Apart from that and the fact that I have nowhere to live and not even the air fare home to see my girlfriend, everything is peachy.'

2 **Alex Higgins**
Snooker player, Alex Higgins, claims that at one stage of his career he was dossing in a row of derelict houses in Blackburn where, he states, he kept just ahead of the bulldozer with five addresses in one week: 9, 11, 13, 15 and 17 Ebony Street.

3 **Emil Zatopek**
Czechoslovakian hero, Emil Zatopek, four times Olympic gold medallist in the 1948 and 1952 games, was cleaning streets in Prague in the mid-1970s.

10 Early Golfing Stages of Severiano Ballesteros

1 At the age of seven, Seve picked up his first golf club but could not afford golf balls and therefore used pebbles from the nearby beach.

2 He started caddying at the age of eight.

3 Two years later he played in his first tournament and came fifth after shooting a nine-hole total of 51.

4 Seve won his first tournament, the local caddy's championship, at the age of twelve. He shot a remarkable 79.

5 At the age of fifteen he won the caddy's championship with a round of 65.

6 The following year Seve became Spain's youngest-ever professional golfer.

7 In 1974 on the European Tour, Seve collected £2,915 in prize money and finished 118th in the order of merit.

8 Two years later, following his first tour success in the Dutch Open and Lancôme Trophy, he was top of the order of merit at the age of nineteen.

9 In 1979 Seve won the British Open at Royal Lytham.

10 At the age of twenty-three, Ballesteros donned his first green jacket, as he won the 1980 US Masters.

The Last 7 Balls of the Most Exciting Test Match ever played

Australia V. West Indies, Brisbane, December 1960

Off the last seven balls, Australia needed six to win with three wickets left.

1st ball One leg bye.
2nd ball Benaud is caught behind for 52.
3rd ball No runs.
4th ball A bye run.
5th ball Single as Wes Hall drops a skier.
6th ball Meckiff pulls ball to mid-wicket boundary where Hunte fields and runs out Grout with his throw. But the batsmen had already run two, so the scores are level with one wicket left.
7th ball A nervous Kline comes into bat, hits his first ball to

Solomon at square-leg who fields and throws the wicket down with one stump to aim at.

Result MATCH TIED.

4 Excuses for Anti-Social Behaviour

1 Money

Yorkshire fast bowler, Paul Jarvis, decided to join the rebels for the 1990 tour of South Africa. He gave the following reason: 'I've got a £60,000 mortgage, a £5,000 overdraft and I'm guaranteed only £10,000 salary from Yorkshire. In the winter I have to fend for myself.'

2 World Peace

The first notable political protest of the post-war Olympics came at Helsinki in 1952 when a 23-year-old girl from West Germany ran into the arena during the opening ceremony, mounted the rostrum, seized the microphone and attempted to deliver a speech on world peace.

3 Cut over the Eye

During the Melbourne Olympics in 1956, Hungary met USSR in a water polo match. Hungary were leading 4–0 when a Russian punched the Hungarian Ervin Zador, cutting him over the eye.

After this incident general brawling in the pool occurred. At one stage three Russians and one Hungarian were ordered out of the action. The Swedish referee ended the match early.

4 The Interests of the Town

In 1971 the Soviet newspaper *Pravda* revealed that a top soccer player, Victor Lysenko of the leading club side of Odessa had used his influence to escape a drink driving charge. His club had pleaded Lysenko's continuing presence in the town side was more important than justice.

'We have to consider the interests of the town and the people,' said a club official.

An Impossible Number of People to count who like a Bet

1 **Jimmy White**
When snooker star Jimmy White was thirteen he went up to his father and asked him if he could borrow some money. His father agreed to let him have thirty shillings. By the end of the day he had turned thirty bob into £1,000, playing money matches, culminating, that night, at Streatham Conservative Club, when he took on one of the top amateurs for a £1,000 stake and won.

2 **New Yorkers**
Horse-racing was stopped in New York in 1905. The target was not so much the sport itself, but rather the evils of excessive gambling. Many racetracks believed that racing would be impossible without bookmakers; courses closed all over the county. But with the introduction of the *Paris Mutuel* betting system, racing gradually became re-established.

5 Facts Ian Botham would rather Forget

1 Botham has twice over-turned a brand new car at a motor-racing track.

2 He has appeared in court accused of assault.

3 Botham once severely cut his hand on a plate-glass window in a pub.

4 He played football for Scunthorpe United shortly before an England tour despite having a suspect knee.

5 Botham has been accused by a New Zealand journalist of taking drugs in his hotel room.

5 Brave Sportsmen

1 and 2 **Colin Cowdrey and Paul Terry**
Colin Cowdrey and Paul Terry have both come out to bat against the West Indies with a broken arm in plaster, Cowdrey in 1963 and Terry twenty-one years later.

3 **Brian Close**
Yorkshire cricket captain, Brian Close, was fielding at short-leg to Martin Young off the bowling of Fred Trueman. Young hit a ball right off the middle of the bat and hit Close on the head. The ball rebounded to first slip who caught it!

As Close went up the pavilion steps at the next interval, a member asked him: 'What would have happened if the ball had hit you slap between the eyes?'

'He'd have been caught at cover', replied the bluff Yorkshireman.

4 **George Foreman**
Boxer/preacher, George Foreman, claimed in January 1990 that he was afraid of nobody. He recalled how once he saved his brother, Robert, from his pet lion! He threw a punch at it. He missed but the beast had seen enough and fled in terror. 'Once you have stood up to a lion you are afraid of nothing.'

5 **Jim Smith**
Jim Smith, a Zambian farmer, swam in a crocodile infested reservoir near his Lusaka home in preparation for the 1990 Commonwealth Games. He commented: 'Perhaps my style is affected, because my head's up all the time looking for crocs!'

8 Sports Stars who are not Desperately Bright

1 **Jimmy White**
Snooker player Jimmy White freely admits that he has hardly ever

read a book and that his writing is unexceptional, but that 'the things I need to do writing-wise, I can.'

2 **Vinny Jones**
'He's incredibly loyal. Ask him to jump off the stand roof and he'd do it. But he's as thick as two short planks. He always grabbed the quiz book on our coach trips so that he could ask the questions. That way he didn't have to answer.'

Annie Reed, physiotherapist at Wealdstone (his first club) on Vinny Jones.

3 **Jim Holton**
'We put bells on a football so he would know where it was. We had complaints from Morris dancers saying he was kicking them all over the place.'

Manager, Tommy Docherty, who bought him for Manchester United.

4 **Tony Knowles**
'I don't think Tony Knowles is ever going to go on "University Challenge".'

Barry Hearn, Snooker impresario, on player Tony Knowles.

5 **Colette Evert**
When Chris Evert Lloyd won the 1981 Ladies' Singles title at Wimbledon her mother Colette exclaimed: 'Chris is on cloud nine. She is, how do you say in England, under the moon.'

6 **Dexter Manley**
After four years at college, Washington Redskin, Dexter Manley, had the reading age of a seven-year-old.

7 **Laura Davies**
Leading British women's golfer, Laura Davies, took five 'O'levels at school and failed them all.

8 **Ian Rush**
Ian Rush, Welsh footballer, said of his move to Italy in 1988: 'It's like going to a different country.'

David Brown's List of Top Ten Sports Broadcasters

1 John Coverdale (BBC Radio 2)
2 Henry Blofeld (Test Match Special, BBC Radio 3)
3 Mike Ingham (BBC Radio 2)
4 The late Peter Jones (BBC Radio 2)
5 Richie Benaud (cricket commentator, BBC TV)
6 Christoper Martin-Jenkins (cricket correspondent, BBC Radio)
7 Desmond Lynam (BBC 'Grandstand' anchorman)
8 Bryan Butler (BBC Radio football correspondent)
9 Peter Allis (Golf commentator, BBC)
10 Graham Goode (Channel 4 racing commentator)

. . . and a special mention for Stuart Hall (maverick football reporter, BBC Radio 2)

4 Sporting Cheats

1 Chalton, the jockey
In 1857 Mr W. L'Anson's Blink Bonny, winner of the Derby and the Oaks, was a hot favourite for the St Leger, but her jockey, Jack Chalton, had been bribed to stop her by John Jackson, one of the leading bookmakers of the town.

The Yorkshire crowd were justifiably furious and gave the filly a hostile reception on her return. The unfortunate L'Anson, who in fact had no part in the plot at all, but had foolishly, despite warnings, trusted his jockey, was nearly lynched, his life being saved by the intervention of Tom Sayers, the prize fighter.

2 James Laming, the binocular man
Jockey Greville Starkey was thrown from his horse Ile de Chypre as he was set to win the King George V Handicap at Royal Ascot in June 1989.

Starkey said: 'All of a sudden the horse veered violently to the left.' Starkey was thrown off the horse. A 'Sonic Gun', invented by a James Laming, disguised as a pair of binoculars, was used to unseat the jockey.

James Laming bragged: 'It was simply a case of raising the binoculars, pressing the trigger and that was it. We knew we had racing at our fingertips. We could hit any race in the world at any time.'

The jury was told: 'This was a conspiracy to undermine the entire system of racecourse betting in the country.'

3 Roberto Rojas
Chilean goalkeeper, Roberto Rojas, was felled by a signal flare thrown from the crowd, during the World Cup qualifier against Brazil in 1984. Rojas was subsequently found to have faked the fall and had inflicted injury upon himself to make it more convincing. Chile were disqualified from the World Cup and Rojas was banned from international football for life.

4 **Bram Stoker, Creator of Count Dracula**
The Dracula writer was disqualified for 'lifting' after winning the 1868 Civil Service 5 Mile Walk Championships in 40.05 minutes.

3 Sporting Coincidences

1 **Centenary Test Match**
Australia's victory of forty-five runs in the Centenary Test match at Melbourne in 1977 was exactly that of their first win in Test matches on the same ground a hundred years earlier.

2 **Saints' player–managers**
In 1942, Alf Ramsey and Harry Evans both signed for Southampton Football Club on the same day. On 9 August 1955 they both became managers for the first time. Ramsey with Ipswich Town and Evans with Aldershot.

3 **Howard Clark**
English golfer Howard Clark was having a Chinese meal in 1985 when he discovered a message in a fortune cookie that read: 'You'll soon be sitting on the top of the world'. Remarkably, two months later he was – he won the individual championship in the World Cup.

The Radio Three Test Match Special Commentary Team

1 John Arlott	*Arl*
2 Trevor Bailey	*Boil*
3 Brian Johnston	*Johnners*
4 Fred Trueman	*Sir Frederick*
5 Don Mosey	*The Alderman*

6 Bill Frindall — *The Bearded Wonder*
7 Henry Blofeld — *Blowers*
8 Christopher Martin-Jenkins — *C.M.J./Jenkers*
9 Robin Jackman — *Jackers*

9 The Counties who contested the first cricket County Championship in 1873

1 Derbyshire
2 Gloucestershire
3 Kent
4 Lancashire
5 Middlesex
6 Nottinghamshire
7 Surrey
8 Sussex
9 Yorkshire

10 Amusing cricketing anecdotes

1 **The unhelpful spectator**
Arthur Mailey was bowling for New South Wales in the famous match in which Victoria scored 1,107 against them. Mailey's figures were 4 for 362. He said afterwards: 'I would have had an even better analysis if a bloke in a brown trilby hat sitting in the sixth row of the pavilion hadn't dropped two catches.'

2 **The educated commentator**
When Tufty Mann, the South African batsman, was giving George Mann, the England captain, a terrible caning, John Arlott, the legendary cricket commentator, described it as a bad case of 'Mann's inhumanity to Mann'.

3 **The bored captain**

Australian cricket captain Warwick Armstrong was once seen reading a newspaper relaxing against a boundary fence during a dull test match at The Oval. Asked how he could explain his behaviour, he replied: 'I wanted to see who we were playing against.'

4 **The confused batsman**

Horace Cameron, the South African batsman, who unfortunately died at the early age of thirty, once hit Yorkshire's Hedley Verity for 30 runs in one over. It was this extraordinary hitting that prompted the well-known quip from wicket-keeper Arthur Wood: 'You've got him in two minds, Hedley. He doesn't know whether to hit you for four or six.'

5 **The batsman with the dilemma**

In 1970 with Glamorgan 11 for 8 against Leicestershire, Don Shepherd greeted Peter Walker at the wicket with the question: 'Shall we put our heads down and make runs or get out quickly and make history?'

6 **Giving vandals a chance**

The great fast bowler, Fred Trueman, was asked by a television interviewer what he would have done with the vandals who tampered with the Headingly wicket during the 1975 Australian Test and his reply was: 'I'd have chucked them off the pavilion on to t'tarmac, but I'm not a cruel man. I'd have given them a fifty-fifty chance. I'd have had Keith Fletcher underneath to catch them.'

7 **The maverick skipper**

Colin Ingleby-Mackenzie, Hampshire's captain in the 1960s, once said: 'I always insist my men are in bed by ten o'clock, after all, play starts at half-past eleven.'

8 **The *double entendre***

On a stop-over in the Middle East, the tour manager, anxious to gain Fred Trueman's confidence, is reported to have said: 'Fred, I hear that the sheikh over here has 198 wives.' The bowler replied: 'Two more, and he can qualify for a new ball.'

9 **The north/south divide**

A southerner who was staying in Leeds decided to watch the annual Roses Match between Yorkshire and Lancashire. Before the game started he found a seat and went off to get a drink, placing his hat neatly on the seat where he had been sitting. On returning a few minutes later he found that his hat had been deposited on to the floor and a large Yorkshireman was sitting on his seat. Somewhat diffidently he spoke up: 'Excuse me, sir, I think you are sitting on my seat. I reserved it with my hat.' The Yorkshireman was unimpressed. 'I'm sorry, lad, it's bums that keep seats up here, not 'ats.'

10 **Yet another Fred Trueman story**

During a Test series, England were toiling in the heat and the captain approached Fred Trueman to ask him to bowl another spell. 'Come on, England is expecting.'

'So that's why it's called the Mother Country,' Trueman replied.

10 Pieces of Information to help you to become a Darts Bore

1 **Yeoman archers**
The origin of darts most likely goes back to the yeoman archers.

2 **Anne Boleyn**
Anne Boleyn gave a set of darts as a present to King Henry VIII.

3 **Pilgrim Fathers**
The Pilgrim Fathers played darts on the *Mayflower* whilst sailing to America in 1620.

4 **Zeppelins**
Darts were thrown by First World War pilots at German Zeppelins.

5 **Brian Gamlin**
Brian Gamlin from Lancashire invented the darts board and the present numbering system.

6 **Oche**
The word 'oche' (line or board from where you throw) derives from a brewery in the West Country called S. Hockey and Sons, which delivers its beer in crates three feet long. The regulars in the pub, in order to measure the standard throwing length, put down three crates, making nine feet in all – a bit long. The nearest they could come to the established throwing length was with four of the new crates, giving an eight-foot throw, which was until recently the standard distance.

7 ***News of the World***
The first national darts tournament was organized by the *News of the World* in 1927.

8 **'Indoor League'**
Darts took off as a television sport when Yorkshire Television decided to introduce an afternoon series entitled 'Indoor League'.

9 **Televised darts**
The BBC started televising darts in 1977.

10 ***The Sun***
The Sun is really the only national daily that regularly reports on the game.

5 Little known Eastern Bloc Defectors

1/2 **Josif Naghi and Zoltan Elekes**
In 1973, during the Milk Race in Britain, the Rumanian cyclists Josif Naghi and Zoltan Elekes left their comrades in Devon and hitch-hiked to London where they asked to stay in the West.

3 **Vaclav Nedomansky**
In 1974, Czech ice-hockey player Vaclav Nedomansky escaped to the West with his wife and children. He finally settled in Canada.

4 **Walter Lambatus**
In 1976, 22-year-old rower Walter Lambatus said that 'he had left for freedom' after his defection during the Montreal Olympics.

5 **Mircea Simon**
Rumanian boxer Mircea Simon defected to the West in 1978, saying that he had never had any choice in his life. 'I was told that I was going to be a boxer, and I became a boxer.'

5 Unusual Diets

1 **Vassily Alexeev**
In his prime, Vassily Alexeev, World Super Heavyweight Champion weight-lifter from 1970–7, was the most decorated man in the Soviet Union. Weighing in at about thirty-three stone, he breakfasted on a

thirty-six egg omelette. For lunch he had six steaks and twenty pints of beer. For his evening meal he would have the same again.

The Russian Olympic handbook listed his hobby as cooking.

2 **Yeovil Town**

Yeovil Town enjoyed a famous FA Cup run in 1949. They put their success down to a special diet of glucose, eggs and sherry.

3 **John Marks**

Australian tennis player John Marks has an unusual way of tuning up for a big match. He shoots starlings with an air-rifle in the morning.

Marks explains: 'That's my standard breakfast – a bowl of cornflakes and a couple of starlings.'

4 **Milo of Crete**

The Greek writer, Milo of Crete, noted that some unscrupulous athletes consumed massive quantities of goat meat before competitions.

5 **Fijian rugby team**

A young reporter asked a member of the Fijian Rugby Union touring side of 1970 how the team celebrated after a match. 'The winners eat the losers' came the reply.

15 Stars who Liked a Drink

1 **Gunnar Museby**

The Icelandic shot-putter won European gold medals in both the 1946 and 1950 Olympic Games, but unfortunately had a drink problem. He disappeared for some time after his first win. In 1949, he re-emerged to improve his national record to 16.41 metres, but celebrated too enthusiastically and was banned. He was reinstated in time to achieve a second European win in 1950, but in 1951 he was again in trouble for his part in a violent robbery.

2 **Wladyslaw Komar**

The Polish shot-putter, the surprise champion at the 1972 Munich

Olympics, was habitually suspended for excessive drinking. Last heard of he was a successful night-club crooner.

3 Elton John

At the time Elton John was made Chairman of Watford Football Club in the 1970s his friends at the club became concerned about his drinking. Team manager Graham Taylor invited him to Sunday lunch, but when the Taylor family sat down to a nice roast, Elton's plate was empty.

A bottle of brandy was placed in front of the superstar and Taylor told him: 'That's all you want these days, isn't it.'

Supposedly it did the trick.

4 Willie John McBride

On the 1968 British Lions' tour of South Africa, the captain of the 'Wreckers', Willie John McBride, was responsible for throwing a bed out of a seventeenth-floor window of the Old Union Hotel in Pretoria. Unfortunately, the bed was for the hotel manager's personal use.

5 Leicester Fosse XI

Nottingham Forest beat Leicester Fosse 12–0 in a First Division match in 1909. Forest, at the time, were in danger of relegation, and after such a surprise result an inquiry was held. In the official findings it was mentioned that the Fosse players had attended the wedding celebrations of a team-mate on the previous day.

... AND ONE STAUNCH LAGER LOUT

One-legged soccer fan Terry Exelby was banned from Scarborough's terraces for a year in December 1989 after admitting to magistrates that he'd been drunk at the town's ground before their local derby with York City.

Exelby was the first English fan to be arrested during the 1986 World Cup; he was collared immediately he stepped off a flight in Texas on his way to Mexico.

... AND ONE WHO WOULDN'T DO WITHOUT IT

After his humiliating 10–1 defeat by Nigel Bond in the first qualifying round of the 1990 Embassy World Snooker Championship, 20-stone Canadian, Bill Werbeniuk, admitted that: 'There are only two cures for my arm tremor – inderal [a drug] and lager.'

Inderal is a barred drug in the sport and, therefore, Big Bill is authorized to drink in order to alleviate his tremor. Unfortunately, twenty-eight pints of lager and eight large whiskies failed to help him in his match with lowly-ranked Bond.

3 Stars who Admitted to taking Drugs

1 **Ian Botham**
In May 1986 cricketer Ian Botham was banned by the Test and County Cricket Board after admitting in a newspaper article that he used to smoke cannabis.

2 **Ben Johnson**
Ben Johnson, the Canadian who wanted a gold medal more than a world record – 'It's something they can't take away from you' – won the 100 metres at the 1988 Seoul Olympics, but was sensationally stripped of his title when a drug test found anabolic steroids in his blood. Johnson was sent home in disgrace.

3 **Kirk Stevens**
On the second day of the 1985 Snooker World Championship, South African Silvino Francisco alleged that in the final of the Dulux Open, five weeks earlier, his opponent Kirk Stevens had been as 'high as a kite, out of his mind with dope'.

Stevens later confessed to his addiction to cocaine on which he estimated he had spent £250,000 over the previous six years.

8 Current Professional Cricketers who went to Durham University

1 Graham Fowler *Lancashire*
2 Paul Allott *Lancashire*
3 Tim Curtis *Worcestershire*

Durham University

4 Gehan Mendis	*Lancashire*
5 Simon Hughes	*Middlesex*
6 Colin Metson	*Glamorgan*
7 John Stephenson	*Essex*
8 Nasser Hussein	*Essex*

7 Sporting Eccentrics

1 **The Japanese golfers**

At the Waika course in Hawaii a terrible delay developed one afternoon. After much discussion the club sent someone out to investigate. The problem concerned four Japanese golfers who had never set foot on a course before; their only experience had been on a driving range. Three of the golfers had lost their balls (they only brought one each) and so they were using the only remaining golf ball. One player would hit his short run after it and mark it and then run back and give the ball to the next who would follow the same procedure.

2 **Zola Budd**

Zola Budd has a poster of American distance runner, Mary Decker, above her bed. Strange really when you consider Zola 'tripped' her in the Los Angeles Olympic 3,000 metres final.

3 **Felix Carvagel**

Felix Carvagel, a Cuban postman, travelled to the 1904 St Louis Olympics only to find the stadium full. The enterprising young man proceeded to undress to his underclothes and gained admission along with the athletes. Unfortunately, his fellow runners lined up for the marathon. The Cuban was allowed to participate with the officials' consent. Along the way he was photographed posing with spectators and even ate breakfast in a restaurant. Unbelievably he managed to finish fourth.

4 **Charles Greene**

American, Charles Greene, bronze medallist in the Mexico Olympics, ran in dark glasses, which he apparently called his 're-entry peepers', worn to prevent him being blinded by his own speed.

... AND ONE I CAN'T REALLY UNDERSTAND

American golfer, Mac O'Grady, who incidentally plays right-handed from tee to green and putts left-handed, is the extrovert of the US Tour. He was once asked: 'How did that 65 compare with your 62 in the Greater Harford Open?'

O'Grady replied: 'If you can bring the ship home with cargo and crew intact through the hurricane of the last day, that's an achievement. Right?'

. . . AND ONE WHO REALLY COULDN'T CARE LESS

Oliver Jones, who played prop-forward for the Old Edwardians for an unbelievable but commendable forty-odd years only scored three tries in his entire career. It did not bother this enduring forward for he explained that he only played 'because I couldn't think of anything else to do on a Sunday'.

11 Sportsmen who have met Unfortunate Ends

1 Jose Culberto

Spanish bullfighter Jose Culberto was enjoying the applause of the crowd after 'killing' his last bull of the afternoon in the summer of 1985. Unfortunately, the dying bull staggered to its feet and plunged a horn through the matador's heart, killing him outright.

2 Billy Richardson

Billy Richardson, prolific West Bromwich Albion goalkeeper of the 1930s, collapsed and died whilst playing a charity match, in March 1959.

3 Richard Wertheim

In October 1989, New York appeal judges ended attempts to sue the US Tennis Association for £1.38 million damages by the family of Richard Wertheim, a 60-year-old linesman at the 1983 US Open Junior final, who died when a ball struck by Sweden's Stefan Edberg hit him in the groin. Wertheim fell back and fractured his skull on the hard surface.

4 Lord Mildmay of Flete

Lord Mildmay of *Flete* drowned in May 1950 whilst taking his customary early morning dip at his seaside home in Devon. Mildmay was the leading amateur rider of the post-war years. It is generally thought that cramp caused his death.

5 **Victor Davis**
Seoul Olympics swimming gold medallist, Canadian, Victor Davis, was run down by a car in November 1989 at the age of twenty-five.

6 **J. W. M. T. Douglas**
J. W. M. T. Douglas, former captain of Essex and an England cricketer, died in December 1930, drowned at sea after a collision of ships in the Kattegart. A survivor said that Douglas could have saved himself but went below to try and rescue his father. He was forty-eight.

7 **Boughera El Oafi**
Boughera El Oafi, the French Algerian, who by coming first in the marathon in 1924 became the first-ever African gold medal-winner, was killed in a family quarrel in 1959.

8 **Steve Profontaine**
US athlete Steve Profontaine, arguably his country's most popular track and field competitor of the early 1970s, was killed in a road accident in Eugene, Oregon, on 30 May 1975 aged just twenty-four.

9 **Michael Decker**
French hammer-thrower, Michael Decker, was shot dead on leaving a young lady's apartment on 6 July 1981, the day after he had been placed third in an international against West Germany.

10 **Hans Woellke**
Hans Woellke, who won the 1936 gold medal at the shot putt, was executed by the French resistance for war crimes in 1943.

11 **Mark Thompson**
Snooker player Mark Thompson committed suicide in November 1984. This was a mysterious case because he appeared to have everything to live for. One day Thompson was alive and apparently happy, the next day he was dead.

7 Sportsmen who have Enjoyed Themselves

1 **Colin Ingleby-Mackenzie and his Hampshire team**
Hampshire cavalier, captain Colin Ingleby-Mackenzie, asserted that when Hampshire first won the championship in 1961 they trained on 'wine, women and song'.

2 **Ray East and his practical jokes**
Essex bowler Ray East, on twelfthman duty at Chelmsford in the 1970s, instead of bringing on soft drinks at the drinks interval brought out champagne.

3/4 **Dennis Lillee and Rodney Marsh**
Dennis Lillee and Rodney Marsh put a rubber snake in umpire Dickie Bird's soup at the lunch interval on the first day of the England–Australia Test Match at Old Trafford in 1981.

5 **Ivanov Vyacheslav**
After winning the gold medal at the 1956 Melbourne Olympics, elated Russian athlete Ivanov Vyacheslav tossed his medal high in the air. Unfortunately, it landed in Lake Wendouree. Despite efforts at recovery the medal was never found.

6 **Barry John**
In 1967, Gareth Edwards and Barry John were both picked for the first time to play for Wales against France. Edwards thought that he had better get in touch with his partner and discuss tactics. 'Don't worry,' came the answer down the phone, 'you throw it and I'll catch it.'

7 **Dawn Fraser**
The great Australian swimmer, Dawn Fraser, four times Olympic gold medallist, was banned for ten years by the authorities after celebrating 'too well' in Tokyo after her third successive gold medal. She and her friends managed to acquire the national flag from Emperor Hirohito's palace.

7 Bizarre Pre-Match Soccer Entertainments Witnessed by Michael Coffey (Roving Football Fan)

1 Karate exhibitions
University College Dublin, Ireland

2 Yodelling display
Inter Bratislava, Czechoslovakia

3 A man running on to the pitch with a stuffed fox to the strains of 'D'ye ken John Peel'
Carlisle United

4 A man dressed as an orange
Arsenal

5 Full Highland pipe band (in a howling gale)
Chorley FC

6 Penalty competition between Merseyside beauty queens
Everton

7 A fox interrupting the pre-match warm up
Dulwich Hamlet FC

3 Important Events in the Cricket World in 1864

1 **Overarm bowling**
Overarm bowling is legalized.

2 ***Wisden***
John Wisden's Almanack is first published.

3 **The doctor**
W. G. Grace played his first major match scoring 170 and 56 not out

for South Wales Club against the Gentlemen of Sussex at the age of sixteen.

4 Notorious Incidents which have called into Question the Ethic of Fair Play

1 **Diego Maradona**

On 22 June 1986 the Aztec Stadium in Mexico City staged the quarter-final of the 1986 World Cup between England and Argentina. Maradona of Argentina, arguably the world's greatest footballer, controversially 'scored' to end the first-half deadlock. It was evident to nearly all the vast world-wide audience that Maradona had knocked in the ball with his hand.

2 **John Dyson**

In cricket, Australian opener, John Dyson, was involved in a controversial incident in Sydney in 1983. During the fifth and final Test against England with the Ashes in the balance, England fast bowler Bob Willis fielded the ball off his own bowling and threw down the stumps with Dyson on nought. Umpire Mel Johnson gave him not out, yet the square leg TV replay showed that the Australian batsman was a good yard short of the crease. Dyson went on to score 79 and Australia drew the match to regain the Ashes.

3 **Jean-Pierre Rives**

French Rugby flanker, Jean-Pierre Rives snatched victory over England with an illegal try at Twickenham in 1981.

The French grabbed a second ball rather than wait for the original ball to be returned from the stands, and took a quick line-out to score a disputed try. A quick line-out is illegal with any other ball than the one last in play. Dickie Jeeps, the RFU President, told the Scottish referee that the original ball had landed in his lap.

4 **Bobby Locke**

During the British Open Golf Championship at St Andrews in 1957, a spectator spotted that the eventual winner, Bobby Locke, had taken his final putt from the wrong position. The Royal and Ancient allowed Locke to keep the title.

12 Fanatical Sports Fans

1 **Chris Silcox**

Night-club owner Chris Silcox from the West Midlands won the Los Angeles Raiders 1989 Supporter of the Year award. On one trip he flew to Philadelphia to see them play and then followed them into Kansas for a second game.

Chris said: 'Most of my friends think I'm crackers, but I was elated when I won the award.'

2 **John Peel**

Radio 1 disc jockey, John Peel, named one of his children after the entire Liverpool squad of that year. Peel insisted that his wife held back on giving birth to their first child until Liverpool were top of the league.

3 **Elvis Costello**

Elvis Costello, pop superstar, is a fanatical Liverpool fan. If one of his concerts coincides with a Liverpool match one of his roadies semaphores the score from the side of the stage.

4/5/6 **Steve Cram, Sebastian Coe, Nigel Kennedy**

All three of these famous people support football teams with a degree of fanaticism. Coe supports Chelsea, Cram supports Sunderland and Kennedy Aston Villa. Unfortunately, I haven't got a story about any one of them.

7 **Two tense unknown fans**

In the Ashes Test Match of 1882 at The Oval the game was so tense on the final day that one spectator died of heart failure whilst another gnawed through his umbrella handle.

8 **Ronald Reagan**

Former US president Ronald Reagan is reported to have put back an important meeting just so he could watch England's own Eddie 'the Eagle' Edwards jump in the Calgary Winter Olympics on television.

9 **Marinski Janeuski**

This retired postman was fined for the murder of his wife and offered a plea of mitigation. He recalled: 'I was watching football on television. My wife attempted to stop me. I strangled her. I always get excited watching football.'

10 **George Dixon**

George Dixon, an Aberdeen football fan based in Australia, listened by phone to the commentary of the 1983 European Cup-Winners' Cup Final. The bill came to £220.

11 **A. Koppite**

A. Koppite, fanatical supporter of Liverpool FC, reportedly once said: 'I love Liverpool so much that if I caught one of their players in bed with my missus I'd tiptoe downstairs to make him a cup of tea.'

12 **Pope John Paul II**

Pope John Paul II has an autographed photograph of footballer Ian Rush in the Vatican.

10 of the Best Named Football Fanzines

1	*Witton Wisdom*	Aston Villa
2	*There's Only One F in Fulham*	Fulham
3	*Dial M For Merthyr*	Merthyr Tydfil
4	*Mission Terminated*	Darlington
5	*The Almighty Brian*	Nottingham Forest
6	*Mo Mo Super Mo*	Montrose
7	*At The End Of The Tunnel*	Dartford
8	*What A Load of Cobblers*	Northampton Town
9	*Only The Lonely*	Airdrie
10	*Fly Me To The Moon*	Middlesbrough

8 Sportmen's Fathers' Occupations

1 John Francome (jockey)	*locomotive fireman*
2 Jack Nicklaus (golfer)	*pharmacist*
3 Payne Stewart (golfer)	*furniture salesman*
4 Roger Taylor (tennis player)	*steelworker*
5 Barry McGuigan (boxer)	*singer* (He was third in the 1970 Eurovision Song Contest)
6 Yves Saint Martin (jockey)	*civil servant*
7 Viv Richards (cricketer)	*prison warder*
8 Geoff Boycott (cricketer)	*miner*

9 Unlikely Cricketing Feats

1 **The Victorian leg-spinner**
T. J. Matthews, the Victorian leg-spinner, is the only man who has taken two hat-tricks in a Test Match. They happened on the same day for Australia v. South Africa at Old Trafford in the 1912 Triangular Tournament.

2 **The hammering**
Australia defeated Nottinghamshire by an innings and 517 runs in two days in June 1921. The match saw C. G. McCartney of Australia score 345 in one day. This is still a record.

3 **The embarrassment**
In 1922, Warwickshire bowled out Hampshire for just 15 runs in their first innings. Amazingly, Hampshire went on to win the match by 155 runs. The scores were: Warwickshire 223 and 158, Hampshire 15 and 521.

4 **In the family**
At Edgbaston in July 1931, Warwickshire played Nottinghamshire. This is the only time in history that a father and son have both made hundreds in the same match, George Gunn and his son George Vivian Gunn.

5 **One for one**
Yorkshire spinner Hedley Verity took ten wickets for ten runs in an innings against Nottinghamshire in 1932.

6 **The big hitter**
Jim Smith of Middlesex was not the world's greatest batsman, but on his day, playing the same stroke to practically every ball, he was a force to be reckoned with.

On 16 June 1938, he really made his mark. He scored fifty in eleven minutes against Gloucestershire. He was out for 66 in eighteen minutes – clean bowled aiming for his ninth six.

7 **The Indian tail-enders**
The Indian last-wicket pair of C. T. Sarwate and J. Banerjee put on 255 together against Surrey in May 1946. This is all the more extraordinary as afterwards they achieved practically nothing in their careers.

8 **The heavy scorer**
J. O. Robertson made an undefeated 331 for Middlesex out of a total of 623 for 5 on the first day of their championship match at Worcester.

9 **The greedy bowler**
Roly Jenkins, a leg-spinner, took two hat-tricks in the same match for Worcestershire against Surrey in August 1949.

. . . AND ONE DREADFUL ANTI-CLIMAX – THE OVAL, 14 JULY 1948

Don Bradman came to the wicket, the crowd rose, the score stood at 117 for 1. It was to be the great batsman's final Test innings. He needed four runs for a Test aggregate of 7,000 runs and an average of one hundred. The England captain, Norman Yardley, gathered his team around him and they gave him three hearty cheers.

Bradman took guard, and successfully played the first ball. The second ball arrived and he played forward, but it was Eric Hollies' googly and he was bowled through bat and pad.

Don Bradman's test average was, therefore, a mere 99.64.

14 Sporting Films

1 Walt Disney's 'The Happiest Millionaire'
Boxing

2 'Five Easy Pieces', starring Jack Nicholson
Bowling

3 'Below The Belt'
Women's wrestling

4 'The Championship Season'
High School basketball

5 'Pauline À La Plage'
Windsurfing

6 'The Great Arsenal Stadium Mystery'
Soccer

7 'Grand Prix'
Motor racing

8 'Champions'
Horse racing

9 'Chariots of Fire'
Athletics

10 'Million Dollar Mermaid'
Swimming

11 'Heaven Can Wait'
American Football

12 'The Natural'
Baseball

13 'Players'
Tennis

14 'This Sporting Life'
Rugby League

13 Notable Firsts

1 **W. H. Smith**
W. H. Smith, former England outside-left, was the first player to score a goal direct from a corner-kick. He did so when playing for Huddersfield Town against Arsenal in 1924. The rule making such a feat possible had only been introduced in the previous game.

2 **Willie Carson**
In 1972, Willie Carson was the first Scotsman to become champion flat race jockey.

3 **Tony Coton**
In 1980, goalkeeper Tony Coton, playing for Birmingham City against Sunderland, saved a penalty with his first touch in first-class football.

4 **One-day cricket**
The first one-day final was between Sussex and Worcestershire for the knock-out competition in September 1963 at Lord's. It was not called the Gillette Cup until 1964.

5 **'One in a million'**
In 1979 history was made when the Helena Springfield Ltd 'One in a million' became the first company-owned horse to win an English Classic when she took the 1,000 Guineas at Newmarket.

6 **Light meters**
Light meters were first introduced in Cricket in 1978 for the Third Test at Lords.

7 **Fred Lillywhite**
From 1848 Fred Lillywhite began taking his own portable printing

press around with him to big matches along with a booth in which to house it. He was the first of many travelling cricket reporters.

8 **Bowlers**
The first time bowlers were given credit for dismissals involving catches and stumpings was in 1836.

9 **Victory**
The West Indies had their first victory over England in 1934.

10 **Commentator**
In 1927, Sir Pelham Warner made the first cricket commentary in England on the match between Essex and the New Zealand touring team at Leyton.

11 **Rachael Heyhoe-Flint**
Rachael Heyhoe-Flint hit the first six by a woman in a Test Match at Lord's in 1952.

12 **Drugs**
The first athlete to die as a result of taking drugs was an Englishman who collapsed and died during the Bordeaux to Paris Cycle Race in 1910.

13 **Ross Jack**
Midfielder Ross Jack scored on his début for the youth team, 'B' team, 'A' team, reserve team and first team at Everton FC. After that single first-team appearance, Everton sold him to Norwich City in 1979.

Football League Division One 1965–6 The Final Placings

1 Liverpool
2 Leeds United
3 Burnley
4 Manchester United
5 Chelsea
6 West Bromwich Albion

7 Leicester City
8 Tottenham Hotspur
9 Sheffield United
10 Stoke City
11 Everton
12 West Ham United
13 Blackpool
14 Arsenal
15 Newcastle United
16 Aston Villa
17 Sheffield Wednesday
18 Nottingham Forest
19 Sunderland
20 Fulham
21 Northampton Town
22 Blackburn Rovers

Football League Division Four 1965–6 The Final Placings

1 Doncaster Rovers
2 Darlington
3 Torquay United
4 Colchester United
5 Tranmere Rovers
6 Luton Town
7 Chester City
8 Notts County
9 Newport County
10 Southport
11 Bradford
12 Barrow
13 Stockport County
14 Crewe Alexandra
15 Halifax Town

16 Barnsley
17 Aldershot
18 Hartlepool United
19 Port Vale
20 Chesterfield
21 Rochdale
22 Lincoln City
23 Bradford City
24 Wrexham

8 Sets of Personalities who are 'Not the Best of Friends'

1 **Hana Mandlikova about Pam Shriver**
'For someone who has such a modest record in the singles game, Pam has much to say.'

2 **Hana Mandlikova about Chris Evert**
'What I am saying is that sometimes her on-camera image can be drastically different to what those of us behind the scenes witness.'

3 **Andre Fabre (trainer) and Cash Assmussen (retained jockey)**
'The two will meet for five minutes before a race and for thirty seconds afterwards. They never mix socially,' an owner states.

4 **Nick Faldo and Sandy Lyle (golfers)**
There is no love lost between Britain's two top golfers, Nick Faldo and Sandy Lyle. One instance of their rivalry took place in the Kenyan Open in 1980. Sandy Lyle decided that the sun's reflection from his putter-head was more than he could bear. Therefore he placed some sticking plaster over the top of the putter and continued with the job.

Faldo, Lyle's playing companion, reported this incident to the officials at the end of the round. Unfortunately, Lyle, by his action was unwittingly in breach of rule 4.2, which states that during a stipulated round, the playing characteristics of a club shall not be purposely changed.

5 **Eric Brown and Tommy Bolt (golfers)**
Eric Brown defeated Tommy Bolt by 4 and 3 in the 1957 Ryder Cup at Lindrick. Bolt refused to shake hands at the end, saying that he hadn't enjoyed the match at all to the American. 'I don't suppose you did!' retorted Brown, 'because you never had an earthly hope of beating me.'

6 **George Emmet and Wally Hammond (cricketers)**
Emmet said of Hammond: 'He was the best of my time, though of course a bastard.'

7 **Don Bradman and Wally Hammond**
In the First Test in Australia in 1946, Bradman had scored 28 when he seemed so obviously caught at second slip that no one at first bothered to appeal. When Bradman didn't move an appeal was finally made. It was turned down. At the end of the over Hammond said to Bradman, 'that's a bloody fine way to start a series.'

Bradman went on to score 187. The two captains hardly spoke again in the course of the series.

8 **Steve Davis and Cliff Thorburn**
Snooker players Steve Davis and Cliff Thorburn have reportedly not spoken to each other since 1979 when in Toronto, Cliff told Steve to relax and not to take the sport so seriously.

6 Interesting Facts about W. G. Grace

1 In his time, W.G. Grace was the second most famous Englishman, the first being William Gladstone.

2 In 1873, W.G. was the first man to do the double of 1,000 runs and 100 wickets. He repeated the achievement for the next five years.

3 In 1876 he scored 839 runs in a week.

4 W.G. captained England at bowls in the first match played at Crystal Palace in 1903 and continued to do so until 1908.

5 W.G. Grace's career details read as follows: just over 55,000 runs, 2,876 wickets and 126 catches.

6 W.G. made his last appearance in 1914 at the age of fifty-eight for Eltham against Grove Park. Typically he top scored in the match making 69 not out.

9 Gifts Given by Sportsmen

1 **A two-iron**
Irishman Christy O'Connor Jnr donated the two-iron club, which he used so effectively to beat Fred Couples in his singles match in the 1989 Ryder Cup match against the United States, to a hospice in Galway. Christy sold the club for £50,000; he did not wish to name the buyer.

2 **Food parcels**
The touring New Zealand cricketers brought over gifts of food parcels to a still rationed England in 1949.

3 **A West Indian cricket cap**

Joel Garner gave umpire Dickie Bird his West Indian cap at the Old Trafford Test in 1984 even after Bird had warned team-mate Malcolm Marshall for intimidatory bowling.

Garner said: 'I want you to have this to remember me. You are a great umpire.'

4 **Touring tie**

Dennis Lillee gave Dickie Bird his official touring tie after the 1975 World Cup with the message – 'Going back to Australia with an open-necked shirt. You can have my tie because you are a great guy and we all think you are a fair umpire.'

5 **Box of golf balls**

When Mr Liang-Hian Lu (Mr Lu) was playing in the 1971 British Open at Royal Birkdale he hooked a ball into the crowd and unfortunately injured a lady spectator who had to be taken to hospital.

Mr Lu visited the lady in hospital and presented her with a box of golf balls and proclaimed: 'Now you throw at me.'

6 **Medals**

Contrary to his media image, Steve Ovett is a man of great generosity. His kindness is illustrated by the fact that he does not keep any of his medals. They go to children in need or as prizes.

7 **Robin Jackman**

Alan Gibson, cricket journalist and broadcaster, notes in his autobiography, *Growing Up With Cricket*, that he has written numerous articles for benefit brochures. He has only been thanked once. He received a letter of encouragement and a bottle of whisky from Robin Jackman.

8 **£100,000**

Nick Faldo, after winning £100,000 for the Suntory World Golf Matchplay Championship in October 1989 donated all the prize money to children's charities.

9 **The football strip**

Coventry footballer David Speedie bought a slick £250 kit for a local Warwickshire pub team in January 1990. But the Maypole side discovered that it didn't, unfortunately, bring an immediate change of luck.

Watched by their benefactor, they lost their first game in their new kit 3–1.

... AND ONE UNWANTED PRESENT

Top boxing promoter Mickey Duff once received a parcel from the Kray twins. It contained four dead rats.

5 Headlines concerning Tony Knowles, Snooker Player

1 'TONY WAS A TURN-ON IN LADIES UNDIES'

2 'IT WAS LUST AT FIRST SIGHT WHEN SHE MET SNOOKER STUD TONY'

3 'HANDSOME HEART-THROB OF THE GREEN BAIZE'

4 'KNOWLES PUTS ON A BRAVE Y-FRONTS'

5 'WHY THEY CALL ME THE HOTTEST POT IN SNOOKER'

3 Hefty Goalkeepers

1 **Willie Foulke**
Football League goalkeeper, William Henry Foulke, born in 1874, at his weighty peak tipped the scales at twenty-four stones. He made 347 League appearances whilst with Sheffield United, Chelsea and Bradford City.

2 **Phil Parkes**
At the end of his career, goalkeeper Phil Parkes, of West Ham United and Queen's Park Rangers, weighed in at around fifteen-and-a-half stone.

3 **Thomas Haylock**
In 1977, Thomas Haylock, goakeeper, was dropped from Greentown FC. Greentown's manager said: 'Haylock's game fell to pieces after the team called him "Cheesecake". I know that he weighs twenty stone and that top-of-the-net work upsets him. Nevertheless, he has only let in 107 goals in three matches.'

Before leaving the ground Haylock claimed that he would do all that he could to regain his place.

. . . AND ONE HEFTY CRICKETER
In a village cricket match a very fat batsman came in to bat and as he was taking up his stance at the wicket the local umpire confided to the visiting bowler: 'We have a special rate for him. If you hit him in front it's LBW, if you hit him behind it's a wide.'

6 Sportsmen who Acted Honourably

1 **Fuzzy Zoeller**
US golfer Fuzzy Zoeller dropped out of Houston University because his coach described him as 'crazy'. Fuzzy used to applaud or congratulate opponents for playing a good shot. His coach would tell him off for such behaviour saying it assisted his opponent to relax.

2 **Martin Donnelly**
In 1947, the famous New Zealand cricketer, Martin Donnelly, was fielding captain at Chichester in Sussex when A. P. Doggart was given out leg before and after hitting the ball. Donnelly recalled him to the wicket.

3 **Anne, Duchess of Westminster**
'I would never let my horse run in the Grand National because I adore him, because he is one of the family and because he is much too precious to me.'

4 **Princess Anne**
Princess Anne told pushy cameramen in 1973: 'You cameramen are getting my goat. Horses are very sensitive. They aren't like humans. They don't understand what all the fuss is about.'

5/6 **Ernst Larsen and Sandor Rozsnyoi**
After officials had disqualified Great Britain's Chris Brasher – winner of the 1956 Olympic steeplechase at Melbourne – for interference with other runners, the second and third placed athletes sportingly

claimed that any interference had been purely accidental and had not affected the result.

10 Interesting Horse Racing Facts

1 **Kincsem**
The Hungarian mare Kincsem, foaled in 1874, was unbeaten in fifty-four races.

2 **Fort d'Or**
The tallest horse to race in recorded history is the English owned Fort d'Or standing 18.2 hands (187 cm).

3 **Dragon Blood**
The shortest odds ever quoted on a horse were 10,000–1 on when Dragon Blood was ridden by Lester Piggott in the Premio Naviglio in Milan in 1967.

4 **Man O'War**
In 1920 the American horse Man O'War was three times quoted at odds of 100–1.

5 **Frank Watson**
The youngest jockey ever to ride was Frank Watson who was only nine years and ten months old when he rode his first winner in South Africa at the turn of the century.

6 **Levi Barlingame**
In 1932 Levi Barlingame rode his last race in Kansas at the age of eighty.

7 **Lightest jockey**
The lighest jockey on record was named Kitchener. He was an Englishman and he won the Chester Cup in 1844. He weighed in at 49 pounds. Four years earlier he had weighed in for racing at 35 pounds. He died in 1872.

8 **Dan R. Lasater**
In 1974 owner Dan R. Lasater (USA) had 494 winners which earned him a then record of $3,022,960 in prize money.

9 **Longest-ever horse race**
The longest-ever horse race – held in Portugal – was 1,200 miles. It was won by an Egyptian-bred Arab horse called Emir.

10 **Largest racecourse**
The world's largest racecourse is Newmarket in Suffolk.

6 Mixed Humorous Sporting Anecdotes

1 **The durable champion**
When Jack Nicklaus walked into the Press tent after his remarkable 1986 US Masters victory at Augusta, the 46-year-old announced: 'OK, where do you want me to start, 1959?'

2 **The empty cabinet**
The famed Tommy Docherty managed Wolverhampton Wanderers in 1985. The team, so successful in the 1950s, had hit upon bad times. Docherty summed up their plight: 'I've just opened the trophy cabinet. Two Japanese prisoners of war jumped out.'

3 **The late developer**
Golfer, Lee Trevino, claims that he was twenty-one before he knew 'Manual Labour wasn't a Mexican'.

4 **The bald father**
As a boy, Dick Francis, jockey turned writer, asked his father: 'How did you lose your hair, Dad?'
'It was shot off during the war,' his father replied.

5 **'Holding the hyphen'**
Nick English, one of the Irish Rugby greats, was once asked to account for a famous tackle he'd missed on the England fly-half Phil Horrocks-Taylor. 'Well,' confessed English, 'Horrocks went one way, Taylor went the other – and I was left holding the hyphen.'

6 **The silent princess**

The Princess of Wales suffered an embarrassing moment in November 1989 at the Sports Personality of the Year awards, sponsored by Panasonic. As she was presenting the award to Tony Jacklin on behalf of golfer, Nick Faldo, the sound system broke down. The silence was broken by comedian Frank Carson who piped up, 'Next time we're going to buy Sony.'

4 Sporting Insults

1 **Feminine?**

At a press conference after the French Open Tennis Championships in 1984, Hana Mandlikova was asked by a reporter: 'What did you think of the way Martina played today?'

'It's hard playing against a man . . .'

2 **Not keen on**

Trainer Linda's husband, Jack Ramsden, described bookmakers in 1989 as 'a bunch of whingeing debt collectors'.

3 **Racist**

Liverpool goalkeeper Bruce Grobbelaar was once out training with Howard Gayle, a black Liverpudlian footballer, and decathlete Daley Thompson. Grobbelaar recalls in his 1986 autobiography: 'It was all very serious until I said "Ready, steady, pick up your lips, go." Howard was not at all amused and found nothing to smile about.'

4 **Language problem**

Fred Ayre, former assistant manager at Wigan Athletic, said of a powerful director in 1981: 'You could put his knowledge of the game on a postage stamp. He wanted us to sign Salford Van Hire because he thought he was a Dutch international.'

9 Cricketers who were Killed during the Great War

1 **A. E. J. Collins**
Who once scored 628 in a house match at Clifton College.

2 **Eustace Crawley**
Who had scored hundreds for Harrow against Eton and for Cambridge against Oxford.

3 **John Howell**
Brilliant schoolboy cricketer.

4 **Arthur Jacques**
He had taken 168 wickets for Hampshire in two seasons.

5 **K. L. Hutchings**
Brilliant Kent amateur.

6 **Percy Jeeves**
Warwickshire.

7 **Major J. Booth**
Yorkshire.

8 **Colin Blythe**
Great spin bowler.

9 **Reggie Schwarz**
Excellent South African all-rounder.

6 Left-wingers who played Football for London Clubs and have played Test Match Cricket For England

Patsy Hendren	*Brentford*
Leslie Ames	*Leyton Orient*
John Arnold	*Fulham*
Laurie Fishlock	*Millwall*
Bill Edrich	*Spurs*
Denis Compton	*Arsenal*

8 Cases of Extreme Bad Luck

1 **P. A. Perrin and his 343 not out**
P. A. Perrin scored 343 not out in Derbyshire's first innings against Essex in 1904 and still played on the losing side. The innings contained sixty-eight boundaries, which is still a world record.

2 **Alex Bird and Tudor Line**
What would have been one of the biggest wins on a horse race by any backer was foiled when Tudor Line was beaten by a neck by Royal Tan in the 1954 Grand National.

On the 4 January 1954, professional punter Alex Bird backed Tudor Line to win £1,000 at 3–1 in a chase at Ayr. The horse won by four lengths. He immediately backed the horse to win the Grand National at 50–1. Tudor Line then won a race at Sandown. Bird made another £6,000. He staked this money on at 33–1. On the 3 March, Tudor Line won at Cheltenham at 11–4 and Bird won another £15,000 which went on the horse at 100–8.

All in all Bird stood to win approximately £500,000, but the horse was beaten in the National by the narrowest of margins by Royal Tan.

3 **John Francome and Sunstroke**

John Francome spent the first five days of his honeymoon in Greece in his hotel bed with sunstroke.

4 **H. T. F. Buse and his loss of revenue**

Somerset's H. T. F. Buse chose Somerset v. Lancashire at Bath as his benefit match in June 1953. Unfortunately for Buse the game was all over with 55 minutes of the first day to spare. Lancashire had won by an innings and 24 runs.

5 **Loss of family benefit**

Denis Compton ran out his brother Leslie during Leslie's benefit match in 1957.

6 **The BBC commentator and the lady golfer**

During one of the Colgate Ladies Tournaments at Sunningdale, BBC golf commentator, Alex Hay, was discussing the beautiful qualities of the seventeeth hole with co-commentator Henry Cotton.

'This is a beautiful little hole, don't you think. Henry?'

'Yes,' replied Henry, 'but it was a lot tighter in my day.'

Unfortunately, during this conversation the picture beamed to millions of the television public was the backside of the attractive American golfer, Marlene Floyd.

7 **Edward Harrison and the broken shaft**

Edward Harrison was playing alone at the Inglewood Country Club in Seattle when the shaft of his golf club broke and pierced his groin. He collapsed and bled to death about 100 yards from the ninth tee where the accident occurred.

8 **The Grand National winner and the missing owner**

When the rank outsider Fionavon, a 100–1 outsider, won the 1967 Grand National, his owner was watching one of his other horses at Worcester.

5 Unusual Facts about Boxer Terry Marsh

1 **The actor**
'I want to become the Michael Caine of the nineties' announced Terry Marsh after he was offered a part in a movie in 1987.

2 **He never suffered from epilepsy**
In 1987 it was reported that a doctor had diagnosed that Marsh suffered from epilepsy. Marsh retired from the ring. In fact, Marsh was suffering from hypoglycemia – he had an addiction to Mars Bars. Apparently, he scoffed ten a day when he was in training for a fight.

3 **He actually said this**
In February 1988 Marsh walked out of a medical test arranged for him by the Boxing Board of Control saying: 'Maybe I'm being paranoid – maybe I'm not paranoid, but because I'm not being paranoid doesn't mean they are not after me!'

4 **The Entrepreneur**
He co-owns six betting shops; promoted boxing matches; has an interest in a smoke detector outfit; manages new boxers; makes after dinner speeches; has his own stand up comic act; and occasionally works as a radio commentator and summarizer.

5 **The method actor**
Marsh gives the reason for the breakdown of his marriage: 'I'm a method actor and when I play a part like this I become the person I'm portraying.'

Marsh was playing a bent copper in a movie thriller.

5 Places that have Witnessed Embarrassing Mistakes

1 Twickenham

Arnold Alcock, a very average member of the Guy's Hospital rugby team was extremely surprised when one morning in 1906 he received a letter from the England Rugby Secretary inviting him to play for his country against South Africa at Twickenham.

It was too late to rectify the error when it was discovered that the invitation should have gone to Andrew Blocock of Liverpool. Arnold was on the field earning his first and only international cap.

2 Kingston, Jamaica

To combat bottle throwing by rioting spectators in the England–West Indies Test Match at Kingston, Jamaica in 1968, the police sprayed tear gas on the offenders. Unfortunately, the prevailing wind carried it across the field into the pavilion and even as far as the parliament building causing the Jamaican Cabinet to suspend its sitting.

3 The Headquarters of the Herefordshire Football League

In 1989 the Herefordshire Football League scrapped plans for a 'centenary' dinner-dance . . . after they discovered the league was only ninety years old.

The Football Association's chief executive, Graham Kelly, was to have been the guest of honour at the dinner and 250 tickets had been sold. The cash was refunded.

4 A local cricket ground

A man whose wife was in hospital expecting a baby telephoned one afternoon to see what the news was. By mistake he got the local cricket ground. When he asked what was the latest position, the reply came back: 'There are seven out already, and the last two were ducks.'

5 Sutton Cricket Club

When in England in 1961 the great South African batsman, Graeme Pollock, then a teenager, turned out for the Surrey club, Sutton. He was put in at No. 8 in the batting order. The Sutton captain declared before the young master could have a knock.

4 Sportsmen who are Careful with their Money

1 **Jack Nicklaus (golfer)**
Jack Nicklaus used to go through three gloves a round, but now claims that since he has bought the golf equipment company, Macgregor, he only uses one.

2 **Kenny Dalglish (football manager)**
Former Liverpool manager, Bob Paisley said of his star centre-forward in 1982: 'Kenny Dalglish calls all his goals 'tap-ins' until we come to the end of the season and we are talking money. Suddenly he changes his mind.'

3 **Stan Smith (tennis player)**
The great US tennis player, Wimbledon champion Stan Smith, always took his wallet on court with him.

4 **Roland Mattes (swimmer)**
The great East German swimmer, Roland Mattes, 100 metre and 200 metre backstroke champion at the 1942 Munich Olympics, was rumoured to always hold himself back when he broke a record, knowing that he would be able to improve on the performance and so earn another large bonus.

5 of the Nastiest NFL Players

1 **Hardy 'The Hatchet' Brown** (San Francisco 49ers, 1950s)
In one season 'The Hatchet' caused twenty-one men to be carried off the field. Although he was not a particularly big man, he used to knock out his opponents with a specially devised, charming uppercut off his shoulder pads.

2 **Johnny Sample** (Baltimore Colts, Washington Redskins, New York Jets)
Sample named his autobiography *The Confessions of a Dirty Ballplayer*. He was very proud of his reputation as the dirtiest of them all. His particular favourite misdemeanour was intercepting passes and throwing the ball into the faces of opposing coaches.

3 **Dick Buktus** (Chicago Bears, 1960s and 1970s)
Affectionately nicknamed 'The Animal', Buktus' party-piece was biting opponents. He was once charged with biting a referee.

4 **Les Richter** (Los Angeles Rams, 1950s and 1960s)
Les has the enviable NFL epitaph that he was 'so mean he frightened himself'. The Rams transferred eleven players in order to obtain Richter in a famous trade.

5 **Joe Schmidt** (Detroit Lions, 1950s and 1960s)
Joe was as violent as 'The Animal' but rather more imaginative. He once tore the pants completely off Rams quarter-back Roman Gabriel with his hands and teeth.

17 of the better nicknames

1 'Ebony Antelope' — Jesse Owens (athlete)

2 'Whispering Death'	Michael Holding (fast bowler)
3 'Rustlers'	John Steele (cricketer)
4 'Stainless'	David Steele (cricketer)
5 'The Grinder'	Cliff Thorburn (snooker player)
6 'Polish Rifle'	Ron Vaworski (American footballer)
7 'Old Man Hubert'	Clive Lloyd (cricketer)
8 'The Wombat'	Graham Edie (Rugby League footballer)
9 'The Wild Bull of the Pampas'	Vince Karalies (Rugby League footballer)
10 'The Shy Millionaire'	Jack Simmons (cricketer)
11 'Benson'	John Holder (cricket umpire)
12 'The Croucher'	Gilbert Jessop (cricketer)
13 'The Mighty Atom'	Jimmy Wilde (boxer)
14 'The Head Waiter'	Harry Wragg (jockey)
15 'The Crafty Cockney'	Eric Bristow (darts player)
16 'The Gee Whiz Kid'	Paul Azinger (golfer)
17 'Big Momma' then 'Medium Momma' and now 'Mini Momma'	Joanne Carner (golfer)

12 Unkind Nicknames

1 'The Preston Plumber'	Tom Finney (footballer)
2 'Chenco' (*Bandy Legs*)	Juan Fangio (racing driver)
3 'Dracula'	Ray Reardon (snooker player)

4 'The Shoreditch Sparrow'	Robin Jackman (cricketer)
5 'Snake'	Ken Stabler (American footballer)
6 'Hacksaw'	Jack Reynolds (American footballer)
7 'The Boil'	Trevor Bailey (cricketer)
8 'Big Eric'	Phil Parkes (footballer)
9 'Whitestick'	John Spencer (snooker player – suffers from double vision)
10 'Sands of . . .	Tsuneyuki 'Tommy' Nakajuma (golfer)
11 'The Walrus'	Craig Stadler (golfer)
12 'Poker Face'	Bob Tway (golfer)

5 Stars who have Said No

1 **John Edwards**
Triple jumper John Edwards refused to compete for Great Britain in the European Cup held at Gateshead in the summer of 1989 for religious reasons. This event was due to be held on a Sunday.

2 **Zola Budd**
Zola Budd is deeply religious and strongly observes the Sabbath. She refused to go to a disco with fellow athletes during the Los Angeles Olympics.

3 **John Simpson**
John Simpson, business manager to golfers Nick Faldo and Sandy Lyle, holed in one at the 157-yard eleventh hole at the Chilba Country Club in Tokyo. Since this can be quite expensive if you perform the feat on a Sunday with the clubhouse packed with 250 people, it is possible to insure against it for a very small premium.

Mr Simpson was informed by the manager of the Chilba bar that for a hole in one it was the custom to buy a present for every member of the club, something like a new golf bag with the member's name on the side!

Facing an invoice for something in excess of £15,000, Simpson made his excuses and, not surprisingly, left.

4 **Tom Finney**

In 1952, Tom Finney, the great winger, at the age of thirty was offered £10,000 to play for Palermo in the Italian league. The offer included a car, a villa and a sizeable salary. The Preston North End board asked Finney not to go and he complied with their wishes and refused the move.

5 **Danny Blanchflower**

Ex-Northern Ireland footballer, Danny Blanchflower, is the only footballer to have turned down 'This is Your Life'.

. . . AND ONE WHO WAS TURNED DOWN . . .

Daley Thompson, Olympic gold medallist, was turned down as a footballer by Fulham.

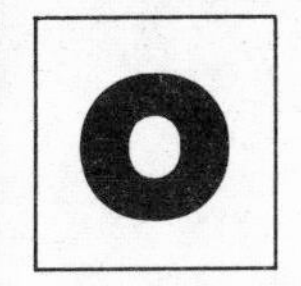

7 Good Reasons for not going to Oklahoma University to play Football

In 1989 the following events occurred:

1 The team were involved in firing a machine gun on the campus.

2 Illegal payments were received by players.

3 There was a scandal concerning the resale of playing tickets.

4 A rough-house was reported involving the team coach.

5 One player was charged with shooting another in the team dormitory.

6 Three undergraduates were charged with rape.

7 The star quarterback was accused of trying to sell cocaine.

The 10 oldest Cricketers to have Captained their Country for the first time in an Ashes Encounter

1	S. E. GREGORY	*Australia*	42
2	T. W. GRAVENEY	*England*	41
3	C. B. FRY	*England*	40
4	W. G. GRACE	*England*	40
5	F. R. BROWN	*England*	39
6	J. RYDER	*Australia*	39
7	A. SHAW	*England*	39
8	J. C. WHITE	*England*	38
9	R. ILLINGWORTH	*England*	38
10	A. L. HASSETT	*England*	37

4 Origins of Indoor Games

1 **Solitaire**

Solitaire developed from a game called 'Fox and Geese' invented by a French nobleman in the 1790s to while away his time in the Bastille.

2 **Dice**

Dice have been found in Egyptian tombs dating back to 2000 BC.

3 **Roulette**

This was first seen in France under the name of 'haca' in about 1655.

4 **Pachisi**

Pachisi is the national game of India. In Britain it is called 'ludo'.

14 Personalities who got it Wrong

1 **Willie Ormond**

Willie Ormond, Scotland manager, said in 1973: 'That Johnny Giles of Leeds is a great player. Beats me why Alf Ramsay has never picked him for England.' Giles played his football for his native Republic of Ireland.

2 **Terry McDermott**

Terry McDermott, ex-Liverpool midfielder, dismissed London's challenge to Liverpool in October 1988 saying: 'Arsenal . . . Spurs? No chance. The two best clubs in London are still Stringfellows and the Hippodrome.' Arsenal went on to win the championship.

3 **Willie Anderson**

The Irish rugby captain, Willie Anderson, said before playing the formidable All Blacks: 'I know the All Blacks are a great side, but we can beat them.' The Irish lost 23–9.

4 **Alan Mullery**

Before the 1980 FA Cup Final, Alan Mullery announced on television that Arsenal would win the game because the Gunners' David O'Leary and Willie Young were in a different class to the Hammers' Alvin Martin and Billy Bonds. West Ham won 1–0.

5 **The Reverend F. H. Gillingham**

The Revd F. H. Gillingham, who during his first BBC commentary stint at The Oval in 1927 was unfortunate enough to have to keep the listeners amused during a fifteen minute rain delay, made the horrendous error of filling in the time reading the various advertisements on the hoardings around the ground.

6 **Barry Hearn**

Impresario, Barry Hearn, said in May 1985: 'Jimmy [White] would be very, very wrong for me and I think my credibility in the industry would suffer if I was with Jimmy.'

In September 1985, the Matchroom boss announced that Jimmy White had become the seventh member of his snooker stable.

7 Mrs Best

In 1980 when George Best went missing again, this time whilst signed to Hibernian, he sought help for his drink problem. His mother offered her support: 'But I'll cut off his legs and put him in a circus if he lets me down.' He did.

8 Jo Durie

British tennis player, Jo Durie, was actually quite successful in the early 1980s, and in 1984 she was ranked five in the world. In fact, Jo was so confident of her ability that she said in February of that year, after having been beaten by Martina Navratilova in the Australian Championships: 'I don't think Martina was so much better than me in Australia. I'm positive I can beat her quite soon.' She hasn't.

9 Frank Bough

Frank Bough, BBC presenter, said in 1977: 'The slalom champion, Stenmark, does not ski downhill.'

10 Seve Ballesteros

Before the 1974 Spanish Open, Seve Ballesteros, a rather arrogant seventeen-year-old, declared that it was impossible for a professional golfer to score double figures on one hole.

The next day, Seve came to the ninth hole on a par five, 586-yard hole. He hooked his drive out of bounds. His second drive, his third shot, was also sliced out of bounds. He eventually reached the fairway in five strokes. His sixth shot dropped into a lake – adding a further one-shot penalty for taking a new ball. He hit this ball into a bunker and finally reached the green in nine shots with two putts and Seve had completed the hole in an 'impossible' eleven.

11 A Misguided Reporter

After a twenty-year-old black American had won the 1964 Olympic Heavyweight boxing gold medal, one reporter wrote: 'A superb left hook but, alas, little else.' He was referring to future World Champion, Joe Frazier.

12 A Bristol Magistrate

A Bristol magistrate told a ten-year-old boy that 'you really must curb this passion for kicking a ball about, otherwise it might get you into trouble.' The boy, Eddie Hapgood, grew up to be an accomplished Arsenal and England footballer.

13 **Ian Botham's headmaster**
Ian Botham's headmaster once described the great cricketing all-rounder as 'a waster'.

14 **Carlo Fassi**
'He's a great skater, but he's a chicken and he won't win the Olympics.'

Carlo Fassi, Robin Cousins' Great Britain coach, said this before Cousins won the gold medal at the Lake Placid Olympics in 1980.

9 Facts about the Great Phar Lap

1 *Phar lap* is Sinhalese for lightning.

2 Many Australians believe he was the greatest racehorse ever foaled anywhere in the world.

3 He was bought at the 1927 New Zealand yearling sales for a mere 160 guineas.

4 As a two-year-old he only won one race from five outings.

5 As a three-year-old he won a staggering thirteen times.

6 Phar Lap as a four-year-old won fourteen races, including the Melbourne Cup.

7 He won his races so easily that for the only time in racing history the conditions of handicapping, weight for age, had to be changed to give other horses a chance of beating him.

8 There was an attempt on his life a few days before his Melbourne Cup success.

9 Sixteen days after easily winning the Agua Caliente Handicap in Mexico in 1931 he was found dead. The cause of his death remains a mystery.

3 Sportsmen who are Pleased with Themselves

1 **Billie Jean King**
'American girls have traditionally looked up to and emulated their favourite motion picture stars. The stars led lives that seemed exciting and far from humdrum, and young girls dreamed of leading similar glamorous lives. Now there is a new idol – and her name is Billie Jean King.'

2 **Eddie 'The Eagle' Edwards**
Not only does Eddie 'The Eagle' Edwards devote an entire chapter in his autobiography to his press cuttings praising his performance at the Calgary Olympics, but he also came out with some remarkably conceited statements. Eddie, the laughably unsuccessful British ski-jumper, wrote of his return to England after the Olympics: 'As the rest of the team collected their luggage and made for the nearest taxi or train home, I was held up by the police who had decided to escort me through the crowd.'

3 **Max Faulkner**
Golfer Max Faulkner started signing his name 'Max Faulkner, the 1951 Open Champion', before the start of the final round of that particular competition. He was right, he won by two shots.

5 American Footballing US Presidents

1 **Franklin Delano Roosevelt**
He captained Harvard's freshman team in 1900.

2 **Dwight D. Eisenhower**
He was a starting Army half-back in 1912 until 12 November, when a broken leg sustained against the Carlisle Indians ended his career. In 1921, Ike coached the Army All-Stars.

3 Gerald Ford
He was Michigan's most prized player in 1934, playing the centre position. (Green Bay Packers offered the 210-pound Ford a professional trial, which he declined.)

4 John F. Kennedy
In 1937–8 J.F.K. was an excellent pass-catching end for the Harvard freshman and junior varsity teams.

5 Ronald Reagan
Ronnie played Prep School ball. As an actor he portrayed Notre Dame's legendary George Gipp in a Warner Brothers movie.

The Crimes for which 8 Stars were sent to Prison

1 High Treason
Charles Hoff, a Norwegian pole vaulter, was convicted for high treason after the Second World War for collaborating with the Nazis.

2 Drugs traffiking
The 1964 100 metres champion, Bob Hayes of the USA, was sentenced at Dallas in March 1979 to five years imprisonment on charges of drugs traffiking.

3 Throwing a punch
Rugby player David Bishop of Pontypool was jailed for a month in September 1986 for knocking out Newbridge forward, Chris Jarman, during a match. Jarman said later: 'I bear no grudge, but I don't think I'll share a pint with him.' Bishop later won an appeal.

4 Tax evasion
The great jockey, Lestor Piggott, was jailed for three years in October 1987 for a £3 million tax fraud.

5 Drink Driving
Liverpool's Danish international, Jan Molby, was jailed in October 1988 for drink driving offences.

6 **Golf course brawl**
At the North West Park Golf Club, Washington, USA, in 1975, fighting broke out between members of two four-ball games. One group claimed that the other was holding them up, the other group claimed the group behind had driven into them. Tempers flared, clubs were raised in anger resulting in serious injuries, including a fractured skull. The police were called and a court case followed.

7 **Attempting to pinch the Argentinian flag**
Irish rugby union captain, Willie Anderson, in 1980 spent four months in an Argentinian jail. He had been caught attempting to steal the national flag. Anderson spent three weeks behind bars with hardened criminals who couldn't speak a word of English. He spent another three months under city arrest before being given a two-year suspended prison sentence.

8 **Umpire battering**
Farokh Muhammad of Winnipeg, Canada, disagreed with an umpire's decision in 1989 and consequently battered the offending umpire unconscious with his bat. He was acquitted of attempted murder but convicted of aggravated assault and possession of a deadly weapon.

4 Successful Punts by Professional Gambler Alex Bird

1 Alex Bird made £5,000 when England won the 1966 World Cup.

2 He made £20,000 after successfully backing Manchester City to win the Football League in 1968–9.

3 Alex Bird backed Derby County to win the 1970–1 First Division championship at various odds of 40–1, 28–1, 16–1, 14–1 and 6–1. He netted £20,000 on this successful investment.

4 He backed Tromos at 9–4 and 11–4 to win the William Hill Dewhurst Stakes at Newmarket in 1978. The horse won by three lengths – Bird won over £16,000.

7 Famous Missed Putts

1 **Ed Sneed**
American Ed Sneed missed from five feet to win the 1979 US Masters at Augusta, Georgia.

2 **Doug Sanders**
Doug Sanders missed a downhill putt of just three feet to win the 1970 British Open at St Andrews. He lost the play-off to Jack Nicklaus.

3 **Hubert Green**
Hubert Green missed from three feet to tie the 1978 US Masters with Gary Player.

4 **Peter Alliss**
Peter Alliss, now an esteemed broadcaster, represented Great Britain and Ireland in the Ryder Cup at Wentworth in 1953. He missed a short putt against Jim Tarnessa to win his match on the eighteenth green. Great Britain/Ireland lost the match 6½ and 5½.

5 **Penny Grice**
In the 1984 Curtis Cup match at Muirfield, Penny Grice from Yorkshire faced a four-foot putt on the final green to win the last hole, halve the match and ensure a tie. Unfortunately, the ball hit the rim of the hole but stayed out.

6 **Andrew Kirkaldy**
In the 1881 British Open, Kirkaldy playing the fourteenth hole in the final round went to knock in a one-inch putt and missed the ball completely. This air-shot lost him victory, for he eventually tied with Willie Park for the hole and then lost the play off.

7 **Ian Mosey**
In the 1979 South African Open, Ian Mosey, a British professional, stood on the final tee needing a par to win the hole. He holed out in six missing a putt of under a yard to tie the match.

16 Memorable Sporting Quotations

1 **Colin Murphy** (FOOTBALL MANAGER)
'One must not become fantoccincal . . . let us hope we are all able to be pulmonic.'

2 **W. G. Grace** (CRICKET LEGEND)
'When I win the toss on a good pitch, I bat. When I win the toss on a doubtful pitch I think about it a bit and then I bat. When I win the toss on a very bad pitch, I think about it a bit longer and then I bat.'

3 **John Barnes** (LIVERPOOL FOOTBALLER)
'I'm just here to bring some colour to the team.'

4 **W. G. Grace** (STILL A CRICKET LEGEND)
'I don't like defensive strokes, you can only get three out of them.'

5 **George Duckworth** (LANCASHIRE AND ENGLAND CRICKETER)
'He makes more appeals than Dr Barnardo,' someone once said of him.

6 **Sir Neville Cardus** (WRITER)
He described Tom Richardson's (Surrey fast bowler) bowling action as being 'like a great wave on the sea about to break'.

7 **Hubert Green** (US GOLFER)
'Ninety-five per cent of putts which finish short don't go in.'

8 **Jack Fingleton** (AUSTRALIAN JOURNALIST)
Describing Len Hutton's 364 for England against Australia, he said: 'Hutton was far too good a batsman to have played it.'

9 **John Francome** (EX-JOCKEY)
'If anyone ever decided to bug a weighing room, ninety per cent of jockeys would immediately become jobless.'

10 **Woody Hayes** (OHIO STATE AMERICAN FOOTBALL COACH)
'When you pass the ball, three things can happen – and two of them are bad.'

11 **The Queen Mother**
After the tragedy in the 1956 Grand National when Devon Loch collapsed on the run-in when leading, the dowager queen said: 'Well, that's racing I suppose.'

12 **Geoff Boycott (CRICKETER)**
Geoff had this to say when he was sacked by Yorkshire Cricket Club: 'If I don't play, I can always sit at home and count my money.'

13 **Brian Clough (FOOTBALL MANAGER)**
Clough said about footballer Trevor Brooking: 'He stings like a butterfly.'

14 **Ian Rush (FOOTBALLER)**
Before going out to join Juventus in 1987, Rushie said: 'I hardly speak English that well, never mind a foreign language like Italian.'

15 **An unkind sportswriter wrote this in 1985**
'Alex Higgins' fate in life is to attract flying dirt.'

16 **George Best (EX-FOOTBALLER)**
Speaking about Paul Gascoigne in 1988, Best opined: 'He is accused of being arrogant, unable to cope with the press and a boozer. Sounds like he's got a chance to me.'

7 Events Racing would rather Forget

1 **Emily Davidson**
Miss Emily Davidson, a suffragette, threw herself in front of the King's horse at the 1913 Derby. She later died in hospital from her injuries.

2 **First World War**
In 1915 all racing was cancelled owing to the Great War. Newmarket, though, for the sake of the industry, was allowed to hold meetings.

3 **Betting tax**
Winston Churchill, the Conservative chancellor, introduced betting tax in 1926. Novelist and racegoer, Edgar Wallace, said at the time: 'It is designed to kill racing, and in the course of time will have that effect.'

4 **Lightning**
After two days of intense humidity, a thunderstorm broke out on Ascot Gold Cup day in 1955. Two racegoers were struck by lightning and subsequently died. Racing was abandoned for only the second time in Royal Ascot's history.

5 **Manny Mercer**
Jockey Manny Mercer, brother of Joe, was killed in 1959 when he was thrown from his mount, Priddy Fair, before the start of the Red Deer Handicap at the Ascot September meeting. Racing was subsequently abandoned.

6 **Strike**
In 1975, Newmarket stable lads went on strike for more money and pulled jockey Willie Carson from his horse.

7 **Lester Piggott**
Lester Piggott, the world's most famous jockey, was imprisoned for tax evasion in 1987. He was released from Norwich gaol in the autumn of 1988.

10 Cricket Ranks in the Second World War

1 Captain Hedley Verity
2 Flight Sergeant Cyril Washbrook
3 Squadron Leader Les Ames
4 Squadron Leader Bill Edrich
5 Warrant Officer Lyndsay Hassett
6 Lieutenant Doug Wright
7 Flying Officer Keith Miller
8 Flight Lieutenant Wally Hammond
9 Captain George Cheetham
10 Lieutenant Colonel Bill Stephenson

7 Stages in the Relationship between Hana Mandlikova and Jan Sedlak

1 Hana meets Jan over a beer in a Czechoslovakian restaurant in Sydney, Australia.

2 Twelve months later Jan, an Australian citizen, takes Hana, a Czech citizen for a cruise around Sydney Harbour.

3 They start going out seriously with each other and plan to get married in Prague.

4 Jan and Hana are secretly married in 1986.

5 Hana takes up the story: 'There was to follow in my life a period of great happiness. Jan and I spent as much time together as we could and the fact that we were not witnessed in public was a matter of our choice.'

6 The relationship deteriorates at the beginning of 1988. They were divorced later in the year.

7 Hana Mandlikova is now an Australian citizen.

6 Sportsmen with Religious Leanings

1 **Ayrton Senna**
The Brazilian Formula 1 driver enjoys a fierce rivalry with Frenchman Alain Prost. Prost said of Senna in 1989: 'Ayrton has a small problem. He believes he can't kill himself because he believes in God.'

2 **Larry Nelson**
The American golfer Larry Nelson is a born-again Christian and enjoys the position of the chief minister of the US Tour's Bible study group.

3 **Dene O'Kane**
The New Zealand snooker player Dene O'Kane, who is based in England, has his own guru (Guru Maharaji).

4 **Albert Knight**
Cricketer Albert Knight (1872–1946) of Leicestershire and England when he caught a ball prayed publicly to Our Lord. He would also pause to pray when beginning his innings.

5 **Prince de Condé**
During the eighteenth century, the Prince de Condé built the magnificent *Grandes Ecuries de Chantilly* for his highly prized string of racehorses. A firm believer in reincarnation, the Duke was convinced in later life he would return to earth as a thoroughbred and take up residence in his grandiose stables.

6 **Henry Armstrong**
Henry Armstrong – world champion boxer at featherweight, lightweight, welterweight and middleweight – was, in 1951, a Baptist Minister (he was incidentally born on the twelfth day of the twelfth month 1912).

. . . AND ONE CARDINAL WHO LOVES SPORT
'I play squash twice a week, and jogging around Wimbledon Common is a great joy. One day I sighted three nuns ahead, so turned off the side path only to run into three people I knew. Also, I never miss "Match of the Day".' *Cardinal Basil Hume, 1977*

AND ONE POPE DEEPLY CONCERNED ABOUT SPORT
In November 1989, Pope John Paul II when blessing the World Cup trophy in preparation for the 1990 Finals in Rome said: 'We are all worried about the possibility of sport degenerating into behaviour which dishonours high ideals.'

10 of the Richest Prizes in Sport

1	Racing	Breeders Cup Classic	£1,100,000
2	Golf	Sun City Tournament	£630,000
3	Athletics	New York Marathon	£41,000
4	Show jumping	Calgary Grand Prix	£92,000
5	Cycling	Tour de France	£200,000
6	Snooker	World Championship	£120,000
7	Yachting	The Ultimate Race, Australia	£500,000
8	Motor racing	Indianapolis 500	£630,000
9	Boxing	Tyson v. Spinks (June 1989)	£14,000,000
10	Tennis	Grand Slam Cup	£1,300,000

10 Stages in the romance of Mike Tyson and Robin Givens

1 A few minutes before his fight with 'Bonecrusher' Smith on 7 March 1987, Tyson told the writer Jose Torres that he had just seen the most beautiful girl in the world on television – Robin Givens.

2 A few days after the Bonecrusher fight, Tyson asked an actor, John Hearne, to ring Givens' publicist and find out her telephone number. This he did.

3 A week later Tyson calls Givens from London and she replies. He

puts the phone down – terrified. He finally plucked up courage and they spoke for nearly an hour.

4 Tyson decides it's time to meet the girl of his dreams and so with his henchman, Rory Holloway, they get into a car and drive to New York City. They took ten thousand dollars out of the bank and went to Gucci and spent it all. Tyson then realized that he didn't have enough money left to spend on Givens and the banks were closed. They drove home.

5 The following day, Tyson went to the bank and withdrew a few thousand dollars, and dressed entirely in Gucci clothes, flew to California. Unfortunately, he was three hours late and when he got to the appointed restaurant, Givens was on her dessert. But Tyson recalls: 'We hung out that night and I was a complete gentleman.'

6 The following night Tyson took Givens out again and she invited him back to her house where he promptly fell asleep on her legs. Unfortunately, during his deep slumber he drooled over her lovely legs. When he woke up he tried to cover his *faux pas* by trying to return the offending dampness into his mouth. He needn't have worried . . . 'She loved it.'

7 On 16 April 1987, Tyson and Givens are seen for the first time together at a function.

8 Tyson and Givens staying at a friend's house have their first fight. Tyson claims the punch he gave Givens was 'the best punch he had ever thrown'.

9 Tyson discovers Givens is three months pregnant.

10 Two weeks later the perfect couple are married in Father George Clements' house in Chicago.

10 Examples of Early Royal Involvement with Horse Racing

1 **Henry VIII**
In Henry VIII's reign there were Royal studs at Hampton Court, Eltham, Tutbury and Malmesbury. Charles V of Spain once sent him twenty-five beautiful Spanish horses from Cordova.

2 **Elizabeth I**
On the eve of the Spanish Armada, Elizabeth I went racing at Salisbury.

3 **James I**
James I founded Newmarket as a sporting centre.

4 **Charles II**
Charles II came to Newmarket for the first time in 1655 and founded the Newmarket Town Plate which was run on the second Thursday in October. The race is indeed still run at Newmarket. In 1667 the King himself rode the winner.

5 **William IV**
William IV first came racing at Newmarket in 1689 and again his horse, the unlikely named Stiff Dick, won a match on the course.

6 **Queen Anne**
Queen Anne founded the Ascot races. The Queen Anne Stakes always open Royal Ascot. Queen Anne also established the Royal plates to encourage the breeding of staying horses, and won one of them in 1714.

7 **George IV**
George IV at the age of fifty-nine in 1820 instituted the Royal procession at Royal Ascot.

8 **William IV**
William IV knew little about racing, but took an amused interest. The story goes that the King's racing manager did not know which of the King's proven stayers, Fleur-de-Lis, Zinganee or The Colonel should start in the Goodwood Cup of 1830. 'Start the whole fleet,' announced the King. They finished first, second and third.

9 **Queen Victoria**
Queen Victoria did not approve of racing and allowed the Royal Stud at Hampton Court to be dispensed with when she came to the throne.

10 **Edward VII**
Albert Edward, Prince of Wales, the future King Edward VII, founded his own stud at Sandringham in Norfolk in the 1880s and became increasingly involved in racing. The Prince of Wales' first trainer on the flat was the great John Porter.

The Last 10 Rugby League Championship Winners

1980–81 Bradford Northern
1981–82 Leigh
1982–83 Hull
1983–84 Hull Kingston Rovers
1984–85 Hull Kingston Rovers
1985–86 Halifax
1986–87 Wigan
1987–88 Widnes
1988–89 Widnes
1989–90 Wigan

11 Important Dates in the History of Rugby League

1 **1895**
On Thursday 29 August at the George Hotel, Huddersfield, twenty-one clubs attended a meeting and passed the following resolution.

'The Clubs here represented decided to form a Northern Rugby Football Union, and pledge themselves to put forward without delay its establishment on the principles of payment for bonafide broken-time only.'

2 **1898**
The Northern Rugby Football Union declared itself professional. Paradoxically, from the very start, no player was allowed to play if he was not in employment.

3 **1906**
In this year Rugby League underwent historic changes. It was decided that: (*a*) teams should be reduced from fifteen to thirteen players; (*b*) that a tackled player should regain his feet and place or drop the ball on to the ground before playing it with his foot in any direction; (*c*) that a scrum should be formed at the point of kicking if the ball entered touch on the full.

4 **1921**
This year saw the game's first £1,000 transfer when Harold Buck was sold to Leeds. Surprisingly, he never won an England cap.

5 **1935**
The headquarters of the Rugby Football League were officially opened at Chapeltown Road, Leeds, where they have been housed ever since.

6 **1943**
On the 23 January, a Rugby League team actually met a Rugby Union team at Headingley, Leeds. The game was played under Rugby Union rules. Eight thousand people saw Northern Command Rugby League XV defeat Northern Command Rugby Union XV 18–11.

7 **1954**
Bradford's Odsal Stadium was the venue for the Cup replay between Halifax and Warrington. The match attracted the largest attendance at a football match of any type outside London or Glasgow. The official attendance was returned at 102,569. For the record Warrington won 8–4.

8 **1966**
The Rugby League introduced the four-tackle law which revolutionized the game. To be caught in possession on the fourth tackle necessitated a scrum. (In 1972 the rule was extended to six tackles.)

9 **1972**

The Rugby League relieved referees of their time-keeping duties and adopted the hooter-timekeeper system.

10 **1983**

The sin-bin was introduced and the four-point try was adopted in this year. Also, 1983 saw the introduction of the turn-over on the sixth tackle. Consequently, scrums have been reduced to a minimum and the game has become faster.

11 **1987**

The reduction of the First Division into a Super League of fourteen clubs served to enhance the quality of play at the top level.

6 Prolific Sexual Athletes

1 **Charlie Nicholas**
'We talked about football, but really he only wanted to talk about sex . . . . I hear he's not been scoring many goals recently and that's why he's left Arsenal, but all I can tell you is, he certainly scored a hat-trick with me that night.'

Thereze Bazaar, pop singer with Dollar, on a night out with Aberdeen footballer, Charlie Nicholas in 1988.

2 **Wally Hammond**
Eddie Paynter, the Lancashire and England batsman, 1901–1979, was once asked who was the greatest of his time? He replied, 'Wally, my he could shag 'em.'

3 **Steve Smith-Eccles**
National Hunt jockey, Steve Smith-Eccles, calculated once that if he got all the women he had been to bed with and laid them out head to toe they would stretch once round Sandown Park paddock and half-way across to the Silver Ring.

4 **John Conteh**
The controversial boxer was quoted as saying in 1978: 'When reporters ask if sex before a fight affects my performance, I always say "which performance" '.

5 **Seve Ballesteros**
Before his marriage, Seve Ballesteros, the great Spanish golfer, was asked by a prying reporter: 'We understand that you have four girlfriends?'

'Maybe more,' came the reply. 'It's very boring playing the same course every day.'

6 **Mike Tyson**
Mike Tyson, world heavywight boxing champion, claims to have had sex with twenty-four prostitutes somewhere near Philadelphia. He was assisted by his friend Rory Holloway. Tyson recalls, somewhat

touchingly: 'There were twenty-four. We ... those bitches in Philadelphia.'

... AND ONE STAR WITH OTHER THINGS ON HIS MIND
Steve Davis was once quoted as saying: 'If I had to choose between sex and snooker, I'd choose snooker.'

... AND ONE MESSAGE OF CAUTION
French screen goddess Brigitte Bardot told the competing French athletes before the 1968 Mexico Olympics: 'Get there early, rest a few days, train carefully and cut out the romance until you get used to the altitude.'

7 Sportspeople who think Sport is taken too Seriously

1 **Valda Lake**
Valda Lake, ranked 11th in Britain and 258th in the world quit the professional tennis circuit in December 1989 because . . . 'there is no fun and no laughter. The girls are ruthless and I just can't take it anymore . . . sometimes it is nice to be stupid and have a laugh, but that does not happen enough for me. The only thing that counts is winning.'

2 **A West German Student**
During the Munich Olympics in 1972 a young West German student ran into the stadium where the vast crowd were anxiously awaiting the arrival of the marathon runners. The spectators cheered him all the way to the line, before realizing that the real front-runners were not yet in the stadium.

The student explained later: 'The purpose of my act was to protest against the solemnity, seriousness and over-organization of the Games.'

3 **George Gunn**
George Gunn, when playing for Nottinghamshire against Glamorgan, started to walk off the field at half past one under the

impression that it was time for lunch. However, under the conditions for that match, lunch was not due until 2.00 p.m. and he was recalled to continue his innings. The Notts player lifted his bat away from the next delivery and was clean bowled, making no attempt to play the ball.

As Gunn retired to the pavilion, he said: 'You can take your lunch, gentlemen, when you like, but I always take mine at 1.30.'

4 **Vera Nikolic**

Yugoslav athlete Vera Nikolic was expected to win the 800 metres at the Mexico Olympics, but inexplicably she dropped out of her semi-final after only 300 metres, walked out of the stadium and attempted to commit suicide by trying to jump off a bridge.

5 **Elisha Scott**

In the 1920s, there was a great rivalry between legendary Everton goalscorer Dixie Dean and Liverpool goalkeeper Elisha Scott. The story is told that when they once met in the street, Dean nodded in acknowledgement only to see Scott fling himself to the ground to save some imaginary header.

6 **Fred Archer**

When Fred Archer was a young jockey he was seen in a weighing room weeping because he had been unable to ride both winners in a dead heat.

7 **Ben Hogan**

After playing a terrific round of golf his great friend Jimmy Demaret, the 1950s Masters champion, was amazed to see Ben Hogan join him on the practice round.

'For Christ's sake, Ben, nobody ever played better than you did today. You can't birdie every hole?'

Hogan replied, 'Why not?'

8 Instances of taking the whole thing Much too Seriously

1 Lord Glasgow

Lord Glasgow, a prominent nineteenth-century member of the British Jockey Club, took full advantage of the particular clause in the marital contract – 'till death do us part' – and shot all his horses who failed to make the grade.

2 A horse racing stable staff

Some years ago a Newmarket trainer threw a party for his thirty staff, but was so dismayed when they talked shop that he brought on a naked black woman to grab their attention. All she wore was a white turban.

'Look,' said one of the lads, 'it's Lord Derby's colours – black with a white cap.' The other boys laughed and returned to their racing talk.

3 Geoffrey Boycott

On 18 October 1965 when the MCC plane to Australia stopped at Colombo Airport, Sri Lanka, on the way, the seventeen tourists were asked to complete forms for the immigration office. One question was: 'What is the purpose of your visit'. Fifteen answered 'to play cricket'. One put 'holiday' and Boycott put 'business'.

4 Gerry Carr

In 1962, Gerry Carr, former British discus champion, ran in a weightmans relay for University College, Los Angeles, against Stanford University. Unfortunately, running the first leg he got so excited he squeezed the baton so hard it broke.

5 Mike Bagley

In January 1984, amateur footballer Mike Bagley of Bristol, was booked for using bad language. Bagley, though, had his revenge . . . he snatched the referee's notebook and ate it. He was subsequently banned for six weeks.

6 Trevor Francis

Trevor Francis, when he was manager of Queen's Park Rangers, in March 1989 fined midfielder Martin Allen two weeks' wages, which was later halved on appeal, for leaving the team hotel before a match against Newcastle United in order to be at his wife's side when she had their first baby.

Frances said: 'He is a professional footballer. I have never known anything like it.'

7 **Don Thompson**

Don Thompson, who won a walking gold medal in the 1960 Olympics, prepared himself for the gruelling heat of Rome by training every day for eighteen months in his bathroom filled with sufficient heat to generate a gas bill for £9,763. He returned from his triumph to find the gas cut off.

8 **Jack Nicklaus**

When in 1972 Jack Nicklaus was practising his short game in preparation for the open championship, his faithful caddie, Jimmy Dickinson, moved slightly.

Without looking up Nicklaus enquired: 'New shoes, Jim?' Jimmy replied that they were.

'Better put some oil on them. They squeak. I'll be able to hear you moving around when I'm putting.'

Gary Sobers' 6 Sixes

Saturday, 31 August 1968, Glamorgan v. Nottinghamshire, at Swansea

1st six Hit over long-on. The ball cleared the wall and hit a pub.

2nd six Hit over mid-wicket. This time Sobers hit another pub and the ball disappeared down another road.

3rd six Hit over long-off. The ball landed amongst the spectators.

4th six Hit mid-wicket. Again the ball landed amongst the enthralled spectators.

5th six Sobers is caught by Roger Davis at long-off. But the unfortunate Welshman is adjudged to have fallen over the boundary line in making the catch.

6th six Hit mid-wicket. The ball travels down the side street towards the Town Hall.

10 of the most Popular Soccer Songs

1 Cockerel Chorus, 'Nice One Cyril' (Tottenham Hotspur)

2 West Ham United Squad, 'I'm Forever Blowing Bubbles'

3 Lonnie Donegan, 'World Cup Willie'

4 England World Cup Squad 1970, 'Back Home' (reached No. 1)

5 Kevin Keegan 'Head Over Heels In Love' (In June 1979 reached No. 3 in the charts)

6 Arsenal Squad, 'Good Old Arsenal'

7 Manchester United Squad, 'Onward Sexton Soldiers'

8 Glen Hoddle and Chris Waddle (Tottenham Hotspur), 'Diamond Lights' (reached the top ten in 1987)

9 Chelsea Squad, 'Blue Is The Colour'

10 Stoke City Squad, 'We'll Be With You'

9 Sports Stars on their Sport

1 **The complete wreck**
'My back is ruined so I can't sit still for long. The game has given me arthritis in the neck from butting people with my head, and if I walk too much my knees swell'.

Peter Gent, thirty-one, retiring US Pro Footballer, 1973

2 **The depressive**
'There's no fun in soccer anymore. It's all deadly serious. We'll end up playing in cemeteries.'

Terry Venables, footballer, 1973

3 **The confused cynic**
'Jockeys are only really there to win on the ones that aren't meant to win.'

Terry Biddlecome, jockey, 1973

4 **The professional**
'Running for money doesn't make you run fast. It makes you run first.'

Ben Jipcho, athlete, on turning professional in 1974

5 **The mathematician**
'A good darts player who can count always beats a brilliant player who can't.'

Leighton Rees, darts player, 1977

6 **The contented**
'Retire, retire to what? I already fish and play golf.'

Julius Boros, golfer

7 **The clean liver**
'To walk back to the dressing room as weak as a kitten with sweat dripping off you, but with your mind as clear as tomorrow's dawn, is better than five reefers or a trip on LSD.'

John Hopkins, squash player

8 **The cautious**
'In my sport the quick are only listed among the dead.'

Jackie Stewart, motor racing

9 **Mr realistic**
'If you are not prepared for bad luck you wouldn't last five minutes in

racing. But in the end it's the same whoever you are. It's about getting on with the horse.'

John Francome, jockey

The 5 Stages in the Mary Decker/Zola Budd Incident, 3,000 Metres Final, Los Angeles Olympics, 1984

1 With 1,320 metres to go Budd draws level with Decker, who had been leading from the start of the race.

2 Forty metres later Budd is now in front, Decker tries to find a way through on the inside. At the third attempt her right knee hits Budd's left leg.

3 Decker falls after colliding with Budd's leg. Budd looks back in anguish as her idol crashes on to the grass, shouting abuse amidst tears.

4 Budd is disqualified and then reinstated. Decker exclaims to Budd who tried to console her: 'Get out of here! Get out! Just go. I won't talk to you.'

5 The American newspapers decide that Budd is not to blame. Allan Mahmud, respected columnist of the Los Angeles Herald writes that the fans should not have booed Budd and that 'maybe they should apologise to Zola for the shoddy treatment which left her in tears on her way out of the athletes' tunnel.'

Zola has the last word: 'I really felt absolutely certain that I was in no way to blame.'

4 Stars who have Suffered in Car Crashes or from Disabilities

1 **Ben Hogan**
On 2 February 1949, Ben Hogan's car was struck by a Greyhound bus travelling on the wrong side of the road. He was left for dead on the side of the road while his wife was attended to. Less than a year later he was playing competitive golf again.

2 **Dick Francis**
Ex-National Hunt jockey and now top writer, Dick Francis, has to tie his arm to his side before he goes to bed at night because if he doesn't and he gets his elbow above his head while he is asleep, his shoulder dislocates.

3 **Eddie Edwards**
The renowned British ski-jumper, Eddie Edwards, was born with a crooked jaw and also forced to wear very thick glasses from an early age.

4 **Helmut Ducadam**
Goalkeeper, Helmut Ducadam of Dinamo/Steaua Bucharest had all his fingers broken by supporters of deposed premier Ceausescu in December 1989.

6 Sportsmen who found Success Early

1 **Steve Cram**
Steve Cram from Jarrow was the youngest man to run a mile in 3 minutes 50 seconds at the age of twenty in 1981.

2 **Derek Underwood**
In 1963 Kent cricketer, Derek Underwood, became the youngest bowler ever to take 100 wickets in an English cricket season.

3 and 4 Dickie Bird and David Constant
Dickie Bird and David Constant in 1974 became the youngest pair of officials to stand in a test. Dickie was forty and David thirty-two.

5 George Deans
The Chairman of Berwick Rangers, George Deans, was just 21 years old when he took over the reins.

6 Ian Botham
By the time he had reached the tender age of twenty-two Ian Botham had played in seven Test matches, had made three centuries and a fifty and had taken five wickets or more in an innings five times.

7 Cricketing Suicides

1 Arthur Shrewsbury (1856–1903)
He was the greatest professional player of his day. He shot himself in 1903 partly because of illness and partly because, in the words of his *Wisden* obituary, 'the knowledge that his career on the cricket field was over quite unhinged his mind'.

2 F. P. Hardy (d. 1916)
The Somerset all-rounder was found dead on the 9 March 1916 on the floor of a lavatory at King's Cross station with his throat cut and a razor by his side.

3 Albert Trott (1873–1914)
Australian cricketer who played for Middlesex.

4 Andrew Stoddart (1863–1915)
English Test cricketer who played for Middlesex.

5 F.G. Bull (1875–1910)
Essex.

6 G. A. Faulkner (1881–1930)
South Africa.

7 W. H. Scotton (1856–93)
Nottinghamshire.

The 4 Olympic Medallists to have Played Tarzan in the Movies

1 **Johnny Weismuller**

Gold	1924, 1928	100 m Freestyle
Gold	1924	400 m Freestyle

2 **Buster Crabbe**

Bronze	1928	1,500 m Freestyle

3 **Herman Brix**

Silver	1928	Shot

4 **Glen Morris**

Gold	1936	Decathlon

6 Incidents that were not to Everyone's Taste

1 **Blasphemy**
In. 1975, US sports commentator, Dick Schaap, referred to the racehorse Secretariat and Riva Ridge as 'the most famous pair of stablemates since Joseph and Mary'. Schaap later apologized for his lack of taste.

2 **Sexism**
The future president of the International Olympic Committee, Avery Brundage, remarked after the 1936 Berlin Olympics: 'I am fed up to the ears with women as track and field competitors, their charms sink to less than zero, they are ineffective and unpleasing on the track. . . .'

3 **Not to be trusted**

In the marathon at the Stockholm Games of 1912, South Africans Kennedy McArthur and Charles Gitsan were well ahead of the field. On the understanding that McArthur would wait for him, Gitsan stopped for a drink of water. McArthur had other ideas and eventually beat his compatriot by just under a minute to win the gold medal. McArthur said later: 'The important thing was to win, just as the most important thing in life is not the triumph but the struggle. I've always said that the essential thing is to have fought well.'

4 **Ostentatious**

When Sugar Ray Robinson fought Randolph Turpin in London in 1951 he had an entourage of fourteen. He turned skipping into a show business number, and he had a Cadillac with the word 'Sugar' written in the style of his own handwriting on the driver's door.

5 **Indigestible**

In 1989 a greyhound was named 'Swallowed a Cat'. Its name was later changed to 'Westmead Fairy' on the advice of the National Greyhound Racing Club, in its role as the dog racing world's guardian of good taste.

6 **Too busy**

On 29 May 1948, a 'well oiled' Lord Tennyson went to the Australian dressing room and asked an attendant to ask Donald Bradman if he could spare a moment. The attendant returned saying, 'sorry, my Lord, Mr Bradman says he's too busy to see you.' A furious Lord Tennyson then wrote to Bradman admonishing the great batsman for his 'appalling' manners.

Tennyson later said: 'I told him I thought that as a former captain of England and a son of a former Governor General of Australia, he might have seen fit to spare me a moment. I also told him that I had merely wanted to congratulate him and to ask him and Hassett, Brown and Miller to dine with me at White's Club. I was so furious that I added good manners cost nothing.'

4 Historic Sporting Telegrams

1 **Queen Mary to Herbert Jones**
'. . . very sorry indeed to hear of your sad accident caused through the abominable behaviour of a brutal, lunatic, woman.'

Sent by Queen Mary to jockey, Herbert Jones, after the suffragette Emily Davidson incident.

2 **George VI to Gordon Richards**
'I am commanded by the King to express to you his Majesty's hearty congratulations on winning your 247th race, and by this splendid achievement establishing a record in the annals of racing in this country.'

The King's congratulatory telegram to Gordon Richards on achieving a record number of winners for one season.

3 **'Heinz Beanz are Haz Beenz'**
Telegram from Johnny Quirke to Tony O'Reilly, Chairman Heinz Inc., on his recall to the Irish Rugby XV 1970.

4 **Fowler's Match**
Since 1910, Eton v. Harrow cricket matches are generally referred to as 'Fowler's Match'. The Eton schoolboy scored 85 runs and took twelve wickets. A telegram of congratulation was sent to 'Fowler's mother, London' after her son's performance.

3 Reasons why Sportsmen have Lost their Temper

1 **On being given out**
England captain, Keith Fletcher, hit his wicket with his bat when given out during the Bangladesh Test of 1981–2. There was an official apology, but Fletcher lost the captaincy after the tour.

2 **On being pelted with oranges**
In December 1980 West Indian Sylvester Clarke lost his temper in the Fourth Test against Pakistan in Multan when he was pelted with oranges whilst fielding on the boundary. Clarke threw a brick into the crowd and knocked out a spectator. He later apologised.

3 **On drawing**
In 1901, Sheffield United met Southern League Tottenham Hotspur in the FA Cup Final at Crystal Palace. Willie Foulke, United's 24-stone goalkeeper, was so incensed at the nerve of Tottenham in managing a 2–2 draw that he ran naked around the corridors of the Crystal Palace changing rooms swearing retribution.

12 Sportsmen Discuss Themselves

1 **Lee Trevino**
'I've got a bad swing, a bad stance and a bad grip, but my banker loves me.'

2 **Derek Randall**
'It gives me great pleasure to please others with my oddities.'

3 **Willie Foulke**
24-stone goalkeeper, 1874–1916

'Ask the old team if a bit of Little Willie's foolery didn't help chirp them up before a tough match.'

4 **Steve Ovett**
'Perhaps the best thing would be if I ran in black and my opponents in all white.'

5 **Wayne Gretzky**
Leading scorer in the history of the National Ice Hockey League

'I'm lucky, I'm god gifted, and I am the first to admit it.'

6 **Seve Ballesteros**
'In the United States I'm lucky. In Europe I'm good.'

7 **Ian Woosnam**
Tiny, Welsh golfer with reference to the 'Great White Shark', Greg Norman

'Perhaps if I dyed my hair peroxide blond and called myself the great white tadpole, that would help.'

8 **Mike Tyson**
'I was born with this disease. I can't help it. Maybe that's why I'm successful at what I do. It's not scary – it's just that I'm abnormally high-strung. There is another word for it, I forget the scientific name, . . . it's a mania, a manic depression and it's a form of something you're born with.'

9 **Ian Rush**
'I can't go round telling the world how good I am. But I suspect that is what they really want me to say.'

10 **John Francome**
'I guess I was just one of those people who was born lucky.'

11 **Hana Mandlikova**
'I was not – and never will be – the kind of girl who sleeps around.'

12 **Ian Botham**
'It's pathetic, even when playing games with my son I have to win.'

6 Test Bowlers who have been No-Balled for Throwing

1 Tony Lock (*England*)
2 Ian Meckiff (*Australia*)
3 Geoff Griffin (*South Africa*)
4 Charlie Griffiths (*West Indies*)
5 Gary Bartlett (*New Zealand*)
6 Geoff Cope (*England*)

Alex Bird's 10 Tips to the Betting Man

1 A punter must never bet in handicaps. Handicaps are computerized therefore there is less chance of the handicapper making a mistake.

2 Back the horse on the near side in a photo-finish.

3 Do not rely on the times when the field is very small because a false pace can be set as jockeys wait on each other.

4 Do not back horses on the first show unless you are absolutely certain.

5 Don't bet if the going changes from firm to heavy.

6 Back successful apprentice jockeys.

7 Every punter should have a notebook.

8 Do not bet at meetings where the percentage of profit to bookmakers is unfair to punters. For instance, at holiday meetings and grade-three courses, especially in winter when the attendance is sparse.

9 If you are losing, stop betting. If you are winning, increase your stake.

10 Read a proper racing paper for the race timings.

11 English Cricketing Tourists of the United States and Canada in 1859

1 George Parr (captain)	*Nottinghamshire*
2 Jeremy Grundy	*Nottinghamshire*

3	John 'Foghorn' Jackson (Nicknamed because he had the endearing habit of blowing his nose each time he took a wicket.)	*Nottinghamshire*
4	Tom Hayward	*Cambridgeshire*
5	Robert Carpenter	*Cambridgeshire*
6	A. J. 'Ducky' Diver	*Cambridgeshire*
7	William Caffyn	*Surrey*
8	Julius Caesar	*Surrey*
9	Tom Lockyer	*Surrey*
10	John Lillywhite	*Sussex*
11	John Wisden	*Sussex*

2 Dreadful British Football Tragedies in the 1980s

1 **Valley Parade**
Fifty-six fans died in May 1985 when fire swept through the main stand at Bradford City's ground in their final game of the season against Lincoln City. The game should have been a celebration of Bradford's promotion from Division Three.

2 **Hillsborough**
At 3.06 p.m. at Hillsborough, Sheffield, on 15 April 1989, the FA Cup semi-final between Liverpool and Nottingham Forest was halted by a terrible disaster. A sudden rush of late arrivals at the Leppings Lane end, where Liverpool fans were standing, caused a crush against the perimeter fencing. The death toll was a tragic ninety-five.

4 Quotes of Lee Trevino

1 **On the press**
'I can't wait to wake up in the morning, to hear what I have to say.'

2 **On his swing**
'I swing the way I used to, but when I look up the ball is going in a different direction.'

3 **On life**
'I've stopped practising. I've stopped worrying and I've got a new wife who travels with me. If I get any happier, I've got to be in heaven.'

4 **On his heavyweight caddie**
'I always know which side a putt will break, it slopes towards the green Herman is standing on.'

8 Unfortunate Stories that hit the Football Pages in 1971–2

1 The raid

In July 1971 Arsenal Chairman Denis Hill-Wood attacked manager, Don Howe, for taking with him two other members of the club's 'backstage' staff (Wright and Whitehouse). 'Loyalty is a dirty word these days, I suppose. It all just staggers me. There is nothing I can do about what West Bromwich have done in raiding our staff, except just to ignore them.'

2 The attack

On 4 August, Arsenal thrashed the Portuguese champions, Benfica 6–2 in a friendly at Highbury. The Portuguese players attacked referee Norman Burtenshaw, who in turn reported the entire team to UEFA.

3 The dirty match

On 14 December, Tottenham Hotspur won their UEFA Cup tie against Rapid Bucharest 2–0 in a vicious game in Rumania.

After the match the Spurs manager Bill Nicholson said: 'If this is European football, we are better out of it. I haven't seen a dirtier game in thirty years.'

4 The wanton star

On 10 January 1972, George Best was interviewed by United manager, Frank O'Farrell, at Old Trafford. He was ordered to move out of his luxury house and return to digs for the rest of the season. He was also fined two weeks' wages and ordered to train morning and afternoon for the rest of the week.

5 The miscreant fan

A Tottenham Hotspur fan was fined £100 on 18 January and bound over not to visit a football ground for a year.

6 The miscreant corner flag?

After Everton and Crystal Palace's rough cup tie at Selhurst Park on 17 January in which referee, Tommy Dawes, sent off Palace's John

Hughes, Palace Chairman Arthur Wait blamed Everton and the referee for the rough-house. 'It was a diabolical game,' he said, 'and Everton were the culprits. Dawes had a real nightmare, at one stage I thought he was going to book the corner flag.'

7 The miners' strike

On 8 February the Football League decided that because of the miners' strike and possible power cuts, mid-week matches must be postponed or played in the afternoon.

8 The wanton star again

On the 20 May, George Best announced his retirement from football at the age of twenty-six. He said that he was a physical and mental wreck and had been drinking too much during the last four months.

7 Unlikely Dismissals

1 Viv Richards and Joel Garner

When in 1986 Somerset Cricket Club surprisingly sacked West Indian superstars Viv Richards and Joel Garner, Ian Botham threatened to leave unless the board changed their minds. They wouldn't and Botham left to go to Worcestershire. Botham said after the event: 'Sacking Viv Richards is equivalent to sending Shergar to Australia for dog meat.'

2 I. Cruttenden

In a cricket match in 1976 between Wadhurst and Mayfried, T. Cruttenden is recorded as having been 'Shambled out'.

3 Bobby Peel

Yorkshire and England slow left-arm bowler Bobby Peel was well known for enjoying a drink. Unfortunately, he became increasingly dependent on alcohol and his career came to an end when he relieved himself on the field of play in front of his captain, Lord Hawke, shortly before the start of play.

4 Bobby Clampett

The then amateur American golfer, Bobby Clampett, missed the thirty-six hole cut in the 1979 US Open at Inverness, Ohio, and was called out for the third round to act as a marker.

On the first tee, Clampett struck his opening drive 220 yards up the middle of the fairway from a kneeling position. He was then warned that if this behaviour was repeated he would be in serious trouble.

Clampett ignored the warning and later in the round he behaved in similar fashion off the tee and putted between his legs with a wedge.

Clampett was met on the twelfth tee by officials who dismissed him from the course.

5 **J. Southerton**

At a cricket match at The Oval in 1970, J. Southerton left his wicket under the impression that he was out, and nothing, not even the decision of the umpires, could induce him to return to the crease. His name appears in the scorebook: 'J. Southerton, retired. Thinking he was caught – 0.'

6 **M. P. Donnelly**

The New Zealand cricketer, playing for Worcestershire against Middlesex at Leeds in 1948, was hit on the foot by a ball from J. A. Young, which bounced over his head. It struck the ground about a foot behind the stumps and span back and hit his wicket.

7 **Brian Johnston**

Doyen of Radio Three's Test Match Special, Brian Johnston was sacked by BBC Television in 1970 after twenty-four years' service because they wanted a more professional and clinical service.

6 Unusual Sporting Events

1 **The Ugly Men v. The Handsome Men**

At Plymouth in 1867 a cricket match was played between The Ugly men and The Handsome men. The result was a draw.

2 **Cricket on horseback**

The Gentlemen on the Hill and The Gentlemen on the Dale played a game of cricket in 1794. It was strange because they played the game from start to finish on horseback.

3 **The Eagle and the Duck**
Eddie 'The Eagle' Edwards has 'water-skied' with Donald Duck.

4 **The Writers' Cup**
The Writers' Cup is an annual golf match between the golfing press of Britain and America.

5 **Bird's challenge sprint**
In September 1977, there was a race between cricketer, Andy Stovold, and umpire, Dickie Bird, at Bristol after close of play against Northamptonshire. The race was set up by Gloucester Captain, South African Mike Proctor. The race was over 100 yards and Bird had a three-yard start. Bird won the race by at least twenty yards.

6 **The disabled challenge**
At Greenwich Hospital, a home for retired sailors, two teams organized a cricket match. At the end of the day, the winner had won by 103 runs. The losers had all lost one arm and the winners were all one-legged.

The 8 Items Dickie Bird Keeps in his Umpire's Coat and their Uses

1 Six miniature beer barrels – counters.

2 A pair of scissors – for repairs to the ball.

3 Penknife – for removing dirt from spikes.

4 Needle and cotton – sewing.

5 Safety pins – minor tears.

6 A rag – for drying the ball.

7 Chewing gum – not for Dickie, but for the players.

8 Spare ball – in case of loss of shape of the original.

11 Pieces of Completely Useless Information

1 **The only 'J'**
St Johnstone, the Perth soccer club, are the only club in either the Scottish League or the Football League whose name contains the letter 'J'.

2 **The smoker**
When Arbroath beat Bon Accord 36–0 in the record-breaking Scottish Cup tie, the Arbroath goalkeeper smoked his pipe throughout the match.

3 **One a minute**
There are an average eighty-five throw-ins in a first-class football match. Nearly one a minute.

4 **The boy came good**
When Everton and Wales goalkeeper Neville Southall played for Llandudno Swifts, he conceded twelve goals against Porthmadog.

5 **The dim and distant past**
Before 1910, to score a six at cricket you had to hit the ball out of the ground.

6 **Without the party piece**
J. A. Snow and J. H. Wardle took 3,000 wickets between them but never had a hat-trick.

7 **Foreigners**
Fifteen of the twenty-eight players on view in a Leeds versus Halifax Rugby League match in 1985 were Australians.

8 **Where was 'Eddie the Eagle'**
The British ski-jumping championships were discontinued in 1936.

9 **Enlightened age?**
Women cricketers prefer to be referred to as batsmen not batswomen.

10 **Worth waiting for**
Barrie Leadbeatter made his only century for Yorkshire in his 208th innings for them.

11 **Tone death**

Crewe Alexandra are the only British or Irish professional football club who have not issued a club song on vinyl.

The Wilson Family Tree

1 **Grandfather**

F. B. Wilson a triple Cambridge Blue and cricket captain

2 **Father**

P. Wilson *Daily Mirror* cricket writer

3 **Son**

J. Wilson BBC racing broadcaster and writer

10 Yorkshire-born cricketers who have played for another County

1	Willie Watson	*Leicestershire*
2	Jim Laker	*Surrey and Essex*
3	Bill Athey	*Gloucestershire*
4	Ray Illingworth	*Leicestershire*
5	Chris Balderstone	*Leicestershire*
6	'Dickie' Bird	*Leicestershire*
7	Brian Close	*Somerset*
8	Brian Bolus	*Nottinghamshire*
9	Jack Birkenshaw	*Leicestershire*
10	Stephen Rhodes	*Worcestershire*

And 1 Zany Story to end with

At the races one day a racegoer noticed a priest making signs over a horse in the paddock. The horse won! Next race the same ritual happened and the horse duly obliged. The overseeing punter approached the priest and asked him what he was doing.

'I'm blessing him,' said the priest. Watching the priest closely when he did the same thing for the next race the punter rushed to put all his money on the same horse, but the horse collapsed in the middle of the race and died. Shattered the punter approached the priest.

'Father,' he said, 'how is it the first two horses won and not the third?'

The priest looked straight at him and said: 'That's the trouble with you Protestants, you can never tell the difference between a blessing and the last rites.'

Index

Alcock, Arnold (Rugger Player), 55
Alexeev, Vassily (Weight Lifter), 20
Ali, Muhammad (Boxer) 3
Alletson, Edwin (Cricketer) 3
Alliss, Peter (Commentator) 13, 69
Allott, Paul (Cricketer) 23
Ames, Leslie (Cricketer/Footballer) 51, 73
Anderson, Willie (Rugger Player) 68
Anne, Queen (Racehorse Owner) 77
Archer, Fred (Jockey) 83
Arlott, John (Commentator) 15, 16
Armstrong, Henry (Baptist Boxer) 74
Armstong, Warwick (Cricketer) 17
Assmussen, Cash (Jockey) 40
Athey, Bill (Cricketer) 106
Ayre, Fred (Football Manager) 50
Azinger, Paul (Golfer) 58

Bagley, Mike (Amateur Footballer) 84
Bailey, Treavor (Broadcaster) 15, 59
Balderstone, Chris (Cricketer/Footballer) 106
Ballesteros, Seve (Golfer) 1, 2, 7, 8, 64, 81, 94
Banerjee J. (Cricketer) 35
Bardot Brigitte (Actress) 82
Barlingame, Levi (Old Jockey) 47
Barnes, John (Footballer) 70
Bazaar, Thereze (Pop Singer) 81
Benaud, Richie (Cricketer/Broadcaster) 1, 8, 13
Best, George (Footballer) 64, 71, 99, 100
Biddlecome, Terry (Former Jockey) 87
Bird, Alex (Professional Punter) 1, 52, 68, 96
Bird, Dickie (Cricket Umpire) 1, 43, 90, 102, 106
Birkenshaw, Jack (Cricketer) 106
Bishop, David (Rugger Player) 67
Blanchflower, Danny (Footballer/Journalist) 60
Blocock, Andrew (Rugger Player) 55
Blofeld, Henry (Broadcaster) 13, 16
Blythe, Colin (Cricketer) 51
Boleyn, Anne (Present Giver) 19
Bolt, Tommy (Golfer) 41
Bolvs, Brian (Cricketer) 106
Bond, Nigel (Snooker Player) 22
Bonds, Billy (Footballer) 60
Booth, Major J. (Cricketer) 51
Borg, Bjorn (Fallen Tennis Idol) 3
Boros, Julius (Golfer) 87
Botham, Ian (Cricket Hero) 1, 10, 23, 65, 90, 95, 100

Index

Bough, Frank (Broadcaster) 64
Boycott, Geoffrey (Cricketer/Broadcaster) 6, 34, 71, 84
Bradman, Sir Donald (Great Cricketer) 34, 41, 92
Brasher, Chris (Steeplechaser) 46
Bristow, Eric (Cockney Darts Player) 2, 58
Brix, Herman (Shot Putter) 91
Brown, Eric (Golfer) 41
Brown, Freddie (Cricketer) 61, 92
Brown, Hardy (Nasty American Footballer) 57
Brundage, Avery (Sports Administrator) 91
Buck, Harold (Rugger Player) 79
Budd, Zola (Runner) 25, 59, 88
Buktus, Dick (Toothy American Footballer) 57
Bull, F. G. (Cricketer) 90
Burgess, Mark (Cricketer) 6
Burtenshaw, Norman (Football Referee) 99
Buse, H.T.F (Unlucky Cricketer) 52
Butler, Bryan (Broadcaster) 13

Caesar, Julius (Cricketer) 97
Caffyn, William (Cricketer) 97
Cameron, Horace (Cricketer) 17
Cardus, Sir Neville (Writer) 70
Carner, Joanne (Golfer) 58
Carpenter, Robert (Cricketer) 97
Carr, Gerry (Discus Thrower) 84
Carson, Frank (Comedian) 49
Carson, Willie (Jockey) 37, 72
Carvagel, Felix (Postman) 25
Chalton, Jack (Jockey) 14
Charlton, Bobby (Former Soccer Star) 3
Charles II, King (Jockey) 77
Chatfield, Ewan (Cricketer) 6
Cheetham, George (Cricketer) 73
Churchill, Sir Winston (Politician) 72
Clampett, Bobby (Golfer) 100, 101
Clark, Howard (Golfer) 15
Clarke, Sylvester (Cricketer) 94
Clements, Fr George (Priest) 76
Close, Brian (Cricketer) 6, 11, 106
Clough, Brian (Football Manager) 71
Coe, Sebastian (Political Runner) 3, 32
Collins, A. E. J. (Cricketer) 51
Compton, Dennis (Cricketer/Footballer) 52, 53
Compton, Leslie (Cricketer/Footballer) 53
Constant, David (Cricket Umpire) 90
Conteh, John (Boxer) 81
Cooper, Henry (Our 'Enry) 3
Cope, Geoff (Cricketer) 95
Costello, Elvis (Pop Star) 32
Coton, Tony (Footballer) 37
Cotton, Sir Henry (Broadcaster) 53

Cousins, Robin (Ice-Skater) 2, 65
Cowdrey, Colin (Ex England Cricket Captain) 11
Crabbe, Buster (Swimmer) 90
Cram, Steve (Runner) 32, 89
Crawley, Eustace (Cricketer) 51
Crenshaw, Ben (Golfer) 2
Cruttenden, Tim (Eccentric Cricketer) 100
Culberto, Jose (Bullfighter) 26
Curtis, Tim (Cricketer) 23

Dalglish, Kenny (Football Manager) 56
Davidson, Emily (Suffragette) 72
Davies, Laura (Lady Golfer) 12
Davis, Roger (Cricketer) 85
Davis, Steve (Top Snooker Star) 2, 41, 82
Davis, Victor (Swimmer) 27
Dawes, Tommy (Football Referee)
Deans, Dixie (Footballer) 83
Deans, George (Football Chairman) 90
Decker, Mary (Runner) 25, 88
Decker, Michael (Hammer-Thrower) 27
De Conde, Prince (Lunatic) 74
Derby, Lord (Racehorse Owner) 84
Disney, Walt (Cartoonist) 36
Diver, A. J. (Cricketer) 97
Dixon, George (Football Fan) 33
Docherty, Tommy (Football Manager) 12, 48
Doggart, A. P. (Cricketer) 46
Donegan, Lonnie (Singer) 85
Donnelly, Martin (Honourable Cricketer) 46, 101
Duck, Donald (Cartoon Hero) 102
Duckworth, George (Cricketer) 70
Duff, Mickey (Boxing Promoter) 44
Douglas, Jumt (Cricketer) 27
Dyson, John (Cricketer) 31

East, Ray (Eccentric Cricketer) 28
Eddery, Pat (Champion Flat Jockey) 1
Edie, Graham (Rugger Player) 58
Edrich, Bill (Cricketer/Footballer) 52, 73
Edward VII, King (Racing Fanatic) 78
Edwards, Eddie (Ski-Jumper Extraordinaire) 32, 66, 89, 102
Edwards, John (Triple-Jumper) 59
Eisenhower, Dwight (Politician) 66
Elekes, Zoltan (Rumanian Cyclist) 20
Elizabeth I, Queen (Racegoer) 77
Eloafi, Boughera (Marathon Runner) 27
Emmet, George (Cricketer) 41
English, Nick (Rugger Player) 48
Evans, Harry (Football Manager) 15
Evert, Colette (Mother of Chris) 12
Exelby, Terry (Soccer Fan) 22

Fabre, Andre (Racehorse Trainer) 40
Faldo, Nick (Golfer) 40, 43, 49
Fangio, Juan (Racing Driver) 58
Faulkner G. A. (Cricketer) 90
Faulkner, Max (Golfer) 66
Fassi, Carlo (Ice Skating Coach) 65
Fingleton, Jack (Journalist) 70
Finnex, Tom (Footballer) 1, 58, 60
Fishlock, Laurie (Footballer/Cricketer) 52
Fletcher, Keith (Cricketer) 17, 93
Floyd, Marlene (Golfer) 53
Ford, Gerald (Politician) 66
Foreman, George (Boxer/Preacher) 11
Foulke, Willie (Fat Goalkeeper) 45, 94
Francis, Dick (Jockey/Author) 48, 89
Francis, Trevor (Footballer) 84
Francome, John (Jockey/Broadcaster) 34, 52, 70, 88, 95
Francisco, Silvino (Snooker Player) 23
Fraser, Dawn (Swimmer) 28
Frazier, Joe (Boxer) 64
Frinoall, Bill (Cricket Statistician) 16
Fry, C. B. (Cricketer, Politician) 61

Gamlin, Brian (Inventor) 19
Garner, Joel (Generous Cricketer) 43, 100
Gayle, Howard (Footballer) 50
Gent, Peter (American Footballer) 86
George IV, King (Innovator) 77
George VI, King (Royalty) 93
Gibson, Alan (Journalist) 43
Gillingham, Rev F. H. (Broadcaster) 63
Gitsan, Charles (Unfortunate Marathon Runner) 92
Givens, Robin (Actress) 75
Gladstone, Sir William (Politician) 42
Glasgow, Lord (Jockey Club Member) 84
Goodall, Fred (Cricket Umpire) 6
Goode, Graham (Racing Commentator) 13
Grace, Dr W. G. (Legend) 2, 29, 42, 61, 70
Graveney, T. W. (Cricketer) 61
Green, Hubert (Golfer) 69, 70
Greene, Charles (Eccentric Runner) 25
Gregory, S. E. (Cricketer) 61
Gretzky, Wayne (Ice-Hockey Phenomenon) 94
Grice, Penny (Lady Golfer) 69
Griffin, Geoff (Cricketer) 95
Griffiths, Charlie (Cricketer) 95
Grobbelaar, Bruce (Goalkeeping Funnyman) 50
Grout, Wally (Cricketer) 8
Grundy, Jeremy (Cricketer) 96
Gunn, George (Cricketer) 34, 82, 83
Gunn G. W. (Cricketer) 34

Hall, Stuart (Energetic Broadcaster) 13
Hall, Wes (Cricketer) 8
Hammond, Wally (Cricketer) 41, 73, 81
Hapgood, Eddie (Footballer) 65
Hardy, F. P. (Cricketer) 90
Harrison, Edward (Amateur Golfer) 53
Hassett A. L. (Cricketer) 61, 73, 92
Hawke, Lord (Cricketer) 100
Hay, Alex (Golf Commentator) 53
Hayes, Bob (Sprinter) 67
Hayes, Woody (American Football Coach) 70
Haylock, Thomas (Fat Goalkeeper) 45
Hayward, Tom (Cricketer) 97
Hearn, Barry (Snooker Impresario) 12, 63
Hearne, John (Actor) 75
Hendren, Patsy (Cricketer) 52
Henry VIII, King (Darts Player) 19, 77
Higgins, Alex (Controversial Snooker Player) 3, 7, 71
Hill-Wood, Dennis (Football Administrator) 99
Hobbs, Sir Jack (Cricketing Legend) 2
Hoddle, Glen (Footballer/Pop Star) 86
Hogan, Ben (Golfer) 83, 89
Holder, John (Cricket Umpire) 58
Holding, Michael (Cricketer/Broadcaster) 58
Hollies, Eric (Cricketer/Broadcaster) 35
Holloway, Rory (Henchman) 76, 81
Holmes, Percy (Cricketer) 2
Holton, Jim (Footballer) 12
Hopkins, John (Squash Player) 87
Hurrocks-Taylor, Phil (Rugby Player) 48
Howe, Don (Football Manager/Coach) 99
Howell, John (Cricketer) 51
Hughes, John (Footballer) 100
Hughes, Kim (Unsuccessful Australian Cricket Captain) 1
Hughes, Simon (Cricketer/Journalist) 24
Hunte, Conrad (West Indian Cricketer) 8
Hume, Cardinal Basil (Fitness Fanatic) 74
Hussein, Nasser (Cricketer) 24
Hutchings K. L. (Cricketer) 51

Illingworth, Ray (Sagacious Cricketer) 2, 61, 106
Ingham, Mike (Broadcaster) 13
Ingleby-Mackenzie, Colin (Cricketer) 17, 28
Inverdale, John (Broadcaster) 13

Jackman, Robin (Cricketer) 43, 59
Jackson, John (Bookmaker) 14
Jackson, John (Cricketer) 97
Jacques, Arthur (Cricketer) 51
James I, King (Royalty) 77
Janewski, Marinski (Postman) 32

Index

Jarvis, Paul (Cricketer) 9
Jeeps, Dickie (Administrator) 31
Jeeves, Percy (Cricketer) 51
Jenkins, Roly (Cricketer) 35
Jessop, Gilbert (Cricketer) 58
Jipcho, Ben (Runner) 87
John, Barry (Rugger Player) 28
John, Elton (Pop Star) 22
Johnson, Ben (Disqualified Sprinter) 23
Johnson, Brian (Veteran Broadcaster) 2, 15, 101
Jones, Bobby (Golfing Legend) 1
Jones, Herbert (Jockey) 93
Jones, Oliver (Rugger Player) 26
Jones, Peter (Broadcaster) 13
Jones, Vinny (Controversial Cricketer) 12

Karalies, Vince (Rugger Player) 58
Kelly, Graham (Administrator) 55
Kennedy J. F. (Politician) 67
Kennedy, Nigel (Violinist) 32
King, Billy Jean (Tennis Player) 66
Kirkaldy, Andrew (Golfer) 69
Kite, Tom (Golfer) 1
Knight, Albert (Religious Cricketer) 74
Knowles, Tony (Snooker Player) 12
Komar, Wladyslaw (Shot-Putter) 21
Kray, Twins (Gangsters) 44

Lake, Valda (Tennis Player) 82
Laker, Jim (Cricketer, Broadcaster) 106
Lambatus, Walter (Rower) 20
Laming, James (Ingenious Inventor) 14
Larsen, Ernst (Sporting Steeplechaser) 46
Lasater, Dan R. (Racehorse Owner) 48
Leadbeatter, Barry (Cricketer) 103
Lillee, Dennis (Cricketer) 6, 28, 43
Lillywhite, Fred (Cricket Reporter) 37
Lillywhite, John (Cricketer) 97
Lloyd, Clive (Cricketer) 58
Lock, Tony (Cricketer) 95
Locke, Bobby (Golfer) 31
Lockyer, Tom (Cricketer) 97
Louis, Spiridon (Marathon Runner) 4
Lu, Liang-Hian (Gentleman Golfer) 43
Lyle, Sandy (Golfer) 40
Lynam, Desmond (Relaxed Broadcaster) 13

Mahmud, Allan (Journalist) 88
Mailey, Arthur (Cricketer) 16
Mandlikova, Hana (Tennis Player) 40, 50, 73, 95
Manley, Dexter (American Footballer) 12
Mann, George (Cricketer) 16

Mann, Tufty (Cricketer) 16
Maradona, Diego (Much Disliked Footballer) 2, 31
Marks, John (Tennis Player) 21
Marsh, Terry (Boxer) 54
Marshall, Malcolm (Cricketer) 43
Martin, Alvin (Footballer) 63
Martin-Jenkins, Christopher (Broadcaster, Journalist) 13, 16
Mary, Queen (Racehorse Owner) 93
Mattes, Roland (Swimmer) 56
Matthews, T. J. (Cricketer) 34
Meckiff, Ian (Cricketer) 8, 95
Mendis, Gehan (Cricketer) 24
Mercer, Manny (Jockey) 72
Metson, Colin (Cricketer) 24
Miandad, Javed (Cricketer) 6
Mildmay, Lord (Amateur Rider) 26, 27
Miller, Keith (Cricketer) 73, 92
Milo, Of Crete (Writer) 21
Molby, Jan (Footballer) 67
Mosey, Don (Broadcaster) 15
Mosey, Ian (Golfer) 69
Mother, The Queen (Racehorse Owner) 71
Morris, Glen (Decathlete) 91
Muhammad, Farokh (Violent Cricketer) 68
Mollery, Allan (Football Manager) 63
Murphy, Colin (Wordy Football Manager) 70
Museby, Gunnar (Shot-Putter) 21

McArthur, Kennedy (Devious Marathon Runner) 92
McBride, Willie John (Rugger Player) 22
McCartney, C. G. (Cricketer) 34
McDermott, Terry (Footballer) 63
McGuigan, Barry (Boxer) 34

Naghi, Josif (Rumanian Cyclist) 20
Nakajima, 'Tommy' (Golfer) 59
Navratilova, Martina (Tennis Champion) 3, 50
Nedomansky, Vaclav (Czech Ice-Hockey Player) 20
Nelson, Larry (Golfer) 74
Nicholas, Charlie (Footballer) 81
Nicholson, Bill (Football Manager) 83
Nicholson, Jack (Actor) 36
Nicklaus, Jack (Golfer) 34, 48, 56, 85
Nikolic, Vera (Middle Distance Runner) 83

O'Connor, Christy (Generous Golfer) 42
O'Farrell, Frank (Football Manager) 99
O'Grady, Mac (Eccentric Golfer) 25
O'Kane, Dene (Religious Snooker Player) 74
Ormond, Willie (Unfortunate Soccer Manager) 63
Ovett, Steve (Kind Runner) 43, 94
Owens, Jesse (Supreme Athlete) 57

Palmer, Arnold (Popular Golfer) 1
Parkes, Phil (Large Goalkeeper) 45, 59
Parr, George (Cricketer) 96
Paynter, Eddie (Cricketer) 81
Peel, Bobby (Boozy Cricketer) 100
Peel, John (Disc-Jockey) 32
Pele, (Brazilian Soccer Hero) 3
Perrin P. A. (Unlucky Cricketer) 52
Pheidippides, (Ancient Runner) 4
Piggott, Lester (Former Champion Jockey) 1, 3, 47, 67, 72
Pollock, Graeme (Cricketer) 55
Prefontaine, Steve (All-round Athlete) 27
Proctor, Mike (Cricketer) 102
Prost, Alain (Racing Driver) 74

Quaife, W. (Cricketer) 2

Randell, Derek (Cricketer) 4, 94
Ramsay, Sir Alf (Football Manager) 15
Ramsden, Jack (Punter) 50
Reagan, Ronald (Politician) 32, 67
Reardon, Ray (Snooker Player) 58
Reed, Annie (Physiotherapist) 12
Rees, Leighton (Darts Player) 87
Reynolds, Jack (American Footballer) 59
Rhodes, Wilfred (Cricketer) 2
Richards, Sir Gordon (Jockey) 93
Richards, Vivian (Cricketer) 34, 100
Richardson, Billy (Footballer) 26
Richter, Les (Mean American Footballer) 57
Rives, Jean-Pierre (Rugby Player) 31
Robertson, J. O. (Cricketer) 35
Robinson, Sugar Ray (Boxer) 92
Rojas, Roberto (Cheating Goalkeeper) 14
Roosevelt, F. D. (Politician) 66
Rozsnyoi, Sandor (Sporting Steeplechaser) 46
Ryder, J. (Cricketer) 61

Saint-Martin, Yves (Jockey) 34
Sample, Johnny (Brutal American Footballer) 57
Sanders, Doug (Unfortunate Golfer) 69
Sayers, Tom (Prize Fighter) 14
Schaap, Dick (Commentator) 91
Schmidt, Joe (Violent American Footballer) 57
Schwarz, Reggie (Cricketer) 51
Scott, Elisha (Footballer) 83
Scotton, W. H. (Cricketer) 90
Sedlak, Jan (Australian Citizen) 73
Senna, Ayrton (Racing Driver) 74
Shankly, Bill (Celebrated Football Manager) 1
Shaw, A. (Cricketer) 61
Shepherd, Don (Cricketer) 17

Shrewsbury, Arthur (Cricketer) 90
Shriver, Pam (Tennis Player) 40
Silcox, Chris (Night Club Owner) 32
Simon, Mircea (Boxer) 20
Simmons, Jack (Cricketer) 58
Simpson, John (Business Manager) 59
Smith, 'Bonecrusher' (Boxer) 75
Smith, Jim (Farmer) 11
Smith, Jim (Appalling Batsman) 35
Smith, Stan (Tennis Player) 56
Smith, W. H. (Footballer) 37
Smith-Eccles, Steve (Energetic Jockey) 81
Sneed, Ed (Golfer) 69
Snow, J. A. (Cricketer) 103
Sobers, Sir Gary (Cricketer) 85
Southall, Neville (Footballer) 103
Southerton, J. (Cowardly Cricketer) 101
Speedie, David (Footballer) 43
Spencer, John (Snooker Player) 59
Spinks, Michael (Boxer) 75
Stable, Ken (American Footballer) 59
Stadler, Craig (Golfer) 59
Starkey, Greville (Jockey) 14
Steele, David (Cricketer) 58
Steele, John (Cricketer) 58
Stenmark, Ingemar (Skier) 64
Stephenson, Bill (Cricketer) 73
Stephenson, John (Cricketer) 24
Stevens, Kirk (Much Troubled Snooker Player) 7, 23
Stewart, Jackie (Racing Driver) 87
Stewart, Payne (Golfer) 34
Stoddart, Andrew (Cricketer) 90
Stoker, Bram (Walker) 15
Stovold, Andy (Cricketer) 102

Taylor, Graham (Football Manager) 22
Taylor, Roger (Tennis Player) 34
Tennyson, Lord Alfred (Cricketer) 92
Terry, Paul (Cricketer) 11
Thompson, Daley (Decathlete) 50, 60
Thompson, Don (Walker) 85
Thompson, Mark (Snooker Player) 27
Thorburn, Cliff (Snooker Player) 41, 58
Trevino, Lee (Effervescent Golfer) 2, 48, 94, 98
Trueman, Fred (Outspoken Cricketer/Broadcaster) 11, 15, 17, 18
Turpin, Randolph (Boxer) 92
Tway, Bob (Golfer) 59
Tyson, Mike (Boxer) 75, 76, 81, 95

Underwood, Derek (Cricketer) 89

Vaworski, Ron (American Footballer) 58

Venables, Terry (Football Manager) 87
Verity, Hedley (Cricketer) 17, 35, 73
Victoria, Queen (Racing Hater) 78
Vyacheslav, Ivanov (Rower) 28

Waddle, Chris (Footballer) 86
Wales, Princess of (Royalty) 49
Walker, Peter (Cricketer) 17
Walwyn, Peter (Racehorse Trainer) 1
Wardle, Johnny (Cricketer) 103
Washbrook, Cyril (Cricketer) 73
Watson, Frank (Cricketer) 47
Watson, Tom (Golfer) 3
Watson, W. (Cricketer) 106
Weismuller, Jonny (Swimmer) 91
Wertheim, Richard (Linesman) 26
Werbenuik, Bill (Boozy Snooker Player) 22
Westminster, Anne Duchess of (Nobility) 46
White, Jimmy (Snooker Star) 10, 11, 63, 64
White, J. C. (Cricketer) 61
Wilde, Jonny (Boxer) 58
William IV, King (Jockey) 77
Willis, Bob (Cricketer) 31
Wilson, F. R. (Amateur Cricketer) 105
Wilson, J. (Racing Broadcaster) 105
Wilson P. (Journalist) 105
Wisden, John (Writer) 29
Woelke, Hans (Shot-Putter) 27
Wood, Arthur (Cricketer) 17
Woolley, Frank (Cricketer) 2
Woosnam, Ian (Golfer) 95
Wragg, Harry (Jockey) 58
Wright, Doug (Cricketer) 73

Yardley, Norman (Cricketer) 35
Young, J. A. (Cricketer) 101
Young, Martin (Cricketer) 11

Zador, Ervin (Water Polo Player) 3
Zatopek, Emil (Legendary Runner) 7
Zoeller, Fuzzy (Honourable Golfer) 46